THE
LAST
STRAW

*Rediscovering
The Laws of the
Harvest*

by Arthur B. Neyland II

ISBN 0-9767147-0-1

Printed in the United States of America.

CONTENTS

Preface

1	The Lord Works in Mysterious Ways	1
2	How's Things Down on the Farm?	6
3	Sliding into Hell	15
4	Protestants no Longer — Just Tants	20
5	Gospel Lite: *Tastes Great — Less Filling!*	24
6	Law 1: The True Gospel	32
7	The Mirror	38
8	Follow-up or Prop-up?	49
9	Rediscovery Leads to Revival — Part 1	56
10	Rediscovery Leads to Revival — Part 2	65
11	Law 2: Travail Prayer — God's Big Plow	73
12	Buggy Wheat	86
13	Law 3: Total Discipleship — Walking Blamelessly	90
14	Which Way Are We Headed?	100
15	Who's the Enemy?	106
16	The Last Straw	112

Endnotes

DEDICATION

To Keith and Carol Neyland, my father and mother that have been such an encouragement to me in their support and love.

To Janet, my wonderful wife, whose hard work and sacrifice for our family has made it all possible.

To A.J. and Angel, my precious gifts from God.

Special thanks to Tom Garrett—for all your long hours of editing and bringing this book to life!

PREFACE

In the latter twentieth century, American Christians became so focused on the rest of the world that we forgot about our own back yard. It is sobering to think that right now, other countries are sending missionaries to the U.S.A. It's like a slap in the face. Shouldn't we be able to reach our own nation?

During the 1980's I was involved with a ministry team that took the message of Jesus to the streets of America. Whenever we went out, guess what? God showed up with us. We weren't out there by ourselves, and amazing things resulted.

The purpose of this book is to open your eyes to a different level of Christianity and to show you how God is still the same today as He was in the days of the early church. God still wants to work with us, once we actually get out there and start sharing his gospel.

Mark 16:15-20 —

> **And He said unto them, "Go ye into all the world and preach the gospel to every creature.**
>
> **He that believeth and is baptized shall be saved, but He that believeth not shall be damned.**
>
> **And these signs shall follow them that believe in My name: they shall cast out devils; they shall speak with new tongues:**
>
> **They shall take up serpents; and if they drink any deadly thing, it shall not hurt them; they shall lay hands on the sick, and they shall recover."**
>
> **So then after the Lord had spoken unto them, He was received up into heaven, and sat on the right hand of God.**
>
> **And they went forth and preached everywhere, the Lord working with them, and confirming the Word with signs following. Amen.**

Surveys have shown that over seventy-five percent of a local population will never come into a church on their own, other than for weddings and funerals.[1] Hmmmm. That's odd!

We have great things going on in our buildings: we have the presence of God, great worship, exciting speakers, awesome videos...

Unfortunately, Jesus never commanded the unbelievers to come in and check us out. So they're not doing anything wrong, so to speak. Jesus commanded *us* to go — out — there — to them. Go *Ye.* (YOU are a YE!) The Bible says that when *we* go out there, He will work with us, confirming what we say.

With much of Christianity, people are trying to do something *for* God. Alas, what we think is being accomplished for him in our own efforts amounts to little, as Jesus said in John 15:5,

"...for without me ye can do nothing."

God is saying that He wants us to hook up with him, so that we are doing something *with* God. He will then confirm what we are doing, and the results will be beyond anything we can ask or think.

The book of Acts is still being written today. If we will do what they did, we will see what they saw.

1

THE LORD WORKS
IN MYSTERIOUS WAYS

I was once a youth pastor in Great Falls, Montana. One year our church teamed up with another one in town for a winter youth retreat. The other youth pastor and I decided to bring in a highly recommended guest speaker. Fortunately, we didn't know him.

The retreat was at a cabin lodge in Monarch, Montana. My youth group was an interesting bunch, consisting mostly of unsaved kids from non-church homes who were dragged in by their Christian friends. Needless to say, we had a lot of the ruffians and Motley Crew types attending our meetings. I befriended many of them, and most of these young "toughians" were present for this particular youth retreat.

When our guest speaker walked to the front of the room on Thursday that first night, we immediately became aware of a slight problem: he was a nerd. Everything about him was N-E-R-D. The other youth pastor and I exchanged glances as if to say, *"Oh man, how did we come up with him?"*

The worst thing that can ever happen, if you're running a youth retreat, happened next. He said to the waiting audience, "Hi! God said He wasn't going to do anything tonight, but He says that Saturday night He will. Thank you." He then turned the meeting back over to me and sat down.

I am not making this up. There I was, trying to figure out what to do with a full room of teenagers. So, for the next three hours we all played games in the lodge, pretending that everything was wonderful. On Friday night we had our praise & worship time. Afterward, the nerd guy came up again to give us the latest update. "Hi! God said He wasn't going to do anything tonight, but He says tomorrow He is." After this announcement, I was faced with seventy grumbling kids, many of them not saved. It was as though they were thinking:

"Yeah, Art, you were telling us what a great time we were going to have. Saturday night, something exciting had better happen."

Saturday night finally came, and we had praise & worship again. Our guest came to the front and said, "Tonight, God is going to show up. What I want is for everybody to get up and form lines across the lodge." So all these teens lined up and held hands, with most of the boys having never held the hand of another boy in their lives. They all gave me that look, and I knew exactly what they were thinking: *"Don't ever expect us to come again to anything YOU'VE got planned, Art, buddy..."*

As this completely non-spiritual group of teens held hands and watched our speaker skeptically, all of a sudden he looked at the ceiling and started laughing: "He's coming! He's coming!" Now everyone was thinking, *"What a weird, like ultimate dud retreat, man."* Even as the youth pastor, I wasn't the least bit excited. (I was thinking: *"Yeah, let's hope God really is coming, or you're goin', man. I'm gonna blackball you from the youth speaker circuit."*)

Then something very odd happened. One by one, starting with the toughest mockers, the youth began falling down. Boom. Boom. Boom. Suddenly, there was a holy presence in our midst. As they hit the ground they would start crying out to God. Almighty God really did show up, as the man of God had predicted!

There was one very peculiar kid from the other youth pastor's church who was the son of a missionary. Right in the middle of this divine visitation, the missionary kid hit the ground—he balled up and started shaking. Our little nerd speaker walked over and said, *"LLLLEEAVE HIMMMM !!!"* The young man jerked and began to weep profusely. He was instantly set free from demonic activity.

Immediately I began to look at our guest speaker in a different light, as if to say, *"Sir, may I please carry your Bible??"*

What I remember the most was the awe of God there. Jesus in His love and power met us that night. As we prepared to leave the next day after our encounter with God, I noticed one of the tough long-haired guys walking outside with a window scraper. I smiled while watching him fervently scrape a Motley-Crew sticker off his car window. He had met with God!

OH NO, NOT A JESUS FREAK

In 1996 I was finishing my degree at Eastern Washington University. Every day I had a twenty-minute bus ride to school. One day, a guy about my age started a conversation: "Hey, where are you from?"

I said, "Montana."

"Really? I'm from Miles City."

"I'm from Great Falls!"

When two people are going to college in a different state and find out they're from the same general area, a feeling of kinship develops. Immediately we became buddies, and he asked me, "Well, how did you get to Spokane?"

I said, "I'm a born-again Christian, and I came here about ten years ago to be part of a ministry that reaches out to drug addicts and street people."

Immediately his facial expression became somewhat contorted. Then he continued, "Looks like it might rain," even though there wasn't a cloud in the sky.

This is what we all fear in evangelism: a person's reaction to the name of Jesus Christ in a G-rated conversation. Things go smoothly until *that* happens (*"Yeech – a Jesus Freak"*). My new acquaintance abruptly decided he didn't want to know any more about me.

However, as a consequence of him being trapped with me on the same bus every day, we did become friends over the next few months. One day, he actually invited me over to his house. During the visit he said, "You know, Art, that first day in the bus when you said you were a born-again Christian? The first thought that went through my head was, 'What a fruitcake.' But immediately after that, there was another thought that came to my mind, and it said, *'You need to listen to what this guy has to say.'*"

Have you ever wondered what goes on in the brain of an unbeliever when you try to tell him about Jesus? *"This guy is a fruitcake"* — well, he probably does think that, but the good news is that God said He's going to confirm what you are saying with signs following. The sign, in this case, was the voice inside my friend's head telling him to listen, even though he didn't want to.

This wasn't Art the Anointed Evangelist, this was Art-Trying-To-Graduate-From-College. But when we share God's Word, He says He will confirm it. My bus friend eventually gave his life to the Lord. It turned out that his wife was a "closet Baptist" that knew all about being saved, and had never told her husband. This forced her to come out of the closet to say, "Oh yes, I know what Art's talking about." [Wife, I thought you were supposed to love your husband, not let him go to hell!]

UNSAVED CHRISTIAN

One late afternoon after a long day of doing street ministry in Spokane, loving Jesus and sharing the good news of the gospel, our evangelism team went to a restaurant called Pioneer Pies. It often happened that after ministering on the streets all day, we would be extremely fired up for the Lord because we felt free from all the concerns of everyday life. We had finally reached the place where we were walking with God, in tune with the Spirit, and the petty things of this world become as nothing.

When you're sitting in a restaurant and excited about Jesus, it's hard to suddenly become a quiet, "normal" person again. So we were off in our own world at the table talking about the wonderful things God had been doing and getting excited about the Word, doing a sermon to the whole restaurant without realizing it. (Anyone who has gone out for coffee with me knows when I get excited — my voice keeps getting louder.) As we were talking, a man in his forties came over and said,

"I believe I've been a Christian my whole life..." and mentioned he went to a certain denominational church. "But I don't have what you guys have. Can you tell me what the difference is?"

Again, this was in Pioneer Pies, when the official time of ministering was over. We said, "You bet, man! Pull up a chair." We talked to him and expounded the whole gospel. At the end he said, "I'm ready to give my life to the Lord," and he prayed.

As we talked to the man about the Lord, in the booth next to us the waitress kept washing and rewashing the table. Soon I began to wonder how clean that table needed to be.

After about three minutes of praying with this man, I noticed that the waitress had stopped cleaning and was just sitting there. We embraced our newly saved brother, gave him some literature, and sent him on his way. The waitress then came over and said, "You know, I'm a backslidden Christian, but when you were praying with him to get saved, I gave my life back to the Lord."

* * *

Friend, there is a higher realm of Christianity that all believers can experience. I know it, because I've tasted it. It can happen in a mountain lodge, a city bus, or even in a restaurant. The question is, how do we not just do something *for* God, but *with* God? How do we get that same kind of heart for people that Jesus had? If we are willing to do so, we can enter into the power of his end-time harvest.

2

HOW'S THINGS DOWN ON THE FARM?

I had the tremendous opportunity to grow up on a farm and enjoy all that comes with it. One of the main problems with society today, in my opinion, is that we've become too urbanized. There is something so wholesome about having solitude and quiet, listening to the birds and watching God's brilliant sunsets. I was powerfully saved on our farm over twenty years ago as Jesus finally found a place to slow my busy life down and quieted me before Him. It's hard to run from God on the farm—there's nowhere to hide!

Over the years I was drawn to study the Bible in light of evangelism and revival, and began to see parallels between the natural and the spiritual harvest. The first question the Holy Spirit implanted in my heart was, "What does a farmer need to raise a good crop?"

Fertilizer, good soil, water, seed, ground preparation time, the sun, money, and some common sense. Jesus talked a lot about the principles of farming. Read Matthew 9:36-38—

> **But when He saw the multitudes, He was moved with compassion on them, because they fainted, and were scattered abroad, as sheep having no shepherd.**
> **Then said He unto his disciples, "The harvest truly is plenteous, but the labourers are few;**
> **Pray ye therefore the Lord of the harvest, that He will send forth labourers into his harvest."**

It says that when He saw the multitudes, He was moved with compassion on them. If we are to represent Jesus well, we must be moved with compassion as He was. Therefore, the first thing needed by the members of an evangelism team (and I insist on it!) is a right heart. We're not here to be arrogant, self-righteous gonging cymbals.

COMPASSION ENDS WITH PASSION

I've heard many say, "Hey, Art, you preach kind of hard. I don't like how you guys buttonhole people out there. Like, 'Here, recieve Jesus, or you're going to burn!' Why not just show some compassion and love on them?"

My answer is usually this: "Okay, I'll go out with you next week, and I'll learn from what you're doing." Unfortunately, 99 percent of the time the self-appointed, Holy Ghost patrol agent is doing nothing to win the lost! I'm not trying to be sarcastic; I'm just making the point that compassion does not mean sitting around judging how others are attempting to fulfill God's calling, but rather compassion is being moved to action!

Theodore Roosevelt, a man of valiant action, said:

> "It is not the critic who counts. Not the man who points out how the strong man stumbled or where the doer of deeds could have done better. *The credit belongs to the man who is actually in the arena,* whose face is marred by dust and sweat and blood; who strives valiantly; who errs and comes short again and again; who knows the great enthusiasms, the great devotions, who spends himself in a worthy cause, who at the best, knows in the end the triumph of high achievement, and who at the worst, at least fails while daring greatly, so that his place shall never be with those timid souls who know neither victory nor defeat."

This is a telltale indicator of who really loves God and lost humanity — they are doing something about it!

One major hindrance to the successful evangelization of America is that we still have a flower-child Jesus image. Probably the last great move of God in our country was during the hippie movement of the 1960's when the Jesus People emerged. Up until that time, mainstream Christianity was very religious and very legalistic.

I had a grandmother who came out of that era: "Your hair is too long," "You shouldn't drink," et cetera. Yes, we're commanded in the New Testament to not be drunk, and it's good to have a nice haircut. But forty years ago there was too much talk about all the things a Christian couldn't do, but not enough talk about WHO JESUS IS! (You would think that they would have realized that people need to change inwardly before it manifests outwardly — but that is the difference between religion and relationship with Christ!)

The Jesus People ushered in the idea that "Jesus loves you," and that blew a generation away. All they had heard about before was a grouchy, legalistic God who was angry with everything from their hairstyle to their platform shoes! American Christianity had become self-righteous, cold toward people, and indifferent toward those who were hurting. So the Jesus movement was a welcome counterbalance to this spiritually sterile condition.

Unfortunately, the pendulum swung to the opposite extreme. Everything became "Jesus loves you, here's a flower, peace-love-joy and Bobby Sherman." To this day, we're still somewhat caught up in the Flower-Child-Jesus image wearing sandals and a tie-dye robe!

I'm not trying to make fun of the message of God's love, because His love is what changes people's lives. But the compassion of Jesus is grounded in truth. The root of that compassion is *passion*. Passion will motivate you to put your hand on the guy who has leprosy (or AIDS) and say, "Be healed!" when no one else wants to touch him. Compassion allows the little children to come up for you to say, "Sit on my lap, and I'm going to bless you."

Compassion, with the root *passion*, also demands that this same Jesus goes and turns over tables of crooks in his temple. Passion dictates that He stands up on a street corner of a city that didn't repent at the preaching of the gospel and say, ***"This is an evil generation! It's going to be better for Sodom than for you on judgment day!"***

Jesus wasn't subject to mood swings per se, one day blessing children because He was in a cheery mood, and the next day turning over tables because He was having a bad hair day. Everything that Jesus did was out of the same heart of compact-passion, and that can express itself in many ways. That's my Jesus, because He is moved with compassion.

1 Corinthians 13 talks about charity (defined as love-in-action). One characteristic of charity is that it rejoices in the truth. What we've been trying to do for the past twenty years in Christianity is to take the truth out of love by sugar-coating it. But love without truth is not true love! If you marry truth and love, and you marry compassion and passion — the love of the lost along with a zeal for righteousness — you've got something that looks a lot like Jesus. That's what we want! *We want a motive of love backed up by a message of truth.* Proverbs 16:6a —

By mercy and truth iniquity is purged.

That's what will change lives. Matthew 9:38 —

"Pray ye therefore the Lord of the harvest, that He will send forth labourers into his harvest."

GOD IS LOOKING FOR SOME FARMERS

A fundamental question that should be at the foundation of prayer and evangelism is: Who is calling the shots on planet earth? God? Satan? The government? (No wonder we're in trouble.) The Body of Christ? If we can't get this one right, we will *never* experience a maximum yield crop! So, what is your final answer? The last answer is correct.

To illustrate: let's say I give my car title and keys to Jimmy — he now has legal right to my vehicle. But Joe comes and steals away the title and keys from Jimmy. Joe now has legal ownership. But here comes John on the scene and he takes the title and keys from Joe and gives them back to Jimmy.

This is exactly what happened in the Bible account of authority delegation between God and man. Genesis 1:26 —

And God said, Let Us make man in our image, after Our likeness; and let them have dominion over the fish of

the sea, and over the fowl of the air, and over the cattle, and over all the earth, and over every creeping thing that creepeth upon the earth.

Almighty God gave dominion over the earth to man. Satan took the keys of authority away due to the fall of mankind in the Garden of Eden. Thus, Satan became the "god of this world" (2 Corinthians 4:4) and the...

...prince of the power of the air, the spirit that now worketh in the children of disobedience.
(Ephesians 2:2)

With the devil comes all the death, destruction and disease that is still prevalent in the earth today.

But the good news is that God sent His Son into the world to destroy the works of the devil (1 John 3:8) and take back the keys of authority to planet earth (Revelation 1:18). Jesus has now given the keys of authority to his church to establish the kingdom and once again have dominion over all the earth (Matthew 16:19, Luke 19:13). God, through His Son, has taken back what the devil stole and has given His church legal authority to farm His land. As in the titles of Milton's classic poems *Paradise Lost* and *Paradise Regained*, we can take our God-given authority and see the earth begin to look a lot more like heaven.

Yes we, the body of Christ, are calling the shots on planet earth. Matthew 9:38 states that it is the Lord's harvest field. Psalm 24:1 —

The earth is the Lord's and the fullness thereof.

God is actually calling and commissioning us to go and farm his land for him.

When I was a young man, our family leased some land from a neighbor and farmed it for them. A lease actually gives the authority and legal right to farm that land. Now, let's suppose that while I leased the land and farmed it, in a certain year the crop was bad with big weeds all over. The owner would have come to me and asked, "Why did you do such a bad job of farming my land?"

What if I had said, "Well, it's your fault there's not a good crop out there—you own the land"? What would have happened then? Bye-bye, Art. Yes, the other man owned it, but he had given legal authority to me to farm it. If there isn't a good crop in the field, it is because I didn't farm very well!

Do we have a good spiritual crop in America? Can you hear God saying, *"How are things down on the ol' farm, guys?"*

"Well, we've got some weeds growing..."
After the Columbine High School shootings, all the TV news and talk shows were discussing the same thing: *"Whose fault is it? Is it the news media, is it the parents, is it education, bad movies..."* and they would debate this thing to death. The answer is: *it's the church's fault.* Jesus has given us the keys of authority to planet earth. Matthew 16:19—

> **And I will give unto thee the keys of the kingdom of heaven: and whatsoever thou shalt bind on earth shall be bound in heaven: and whatsoever thou shalt loose on earth shall be loosed in heaven.**

God is saying in essence, *"I've given you the lease to farm it. And you believers have the authority to dictate what happens down there."* That is a sobering concept. As the church goes, so goes the world.

Throughout church history, whenever there was a true revival in a nation, the whole moral climate of that nation actually changed. That's supposed to be our job, ushering in the principles of the harvest that change cities and nations, because we, as the Christians, are doing the right things in implementing the Kingdom of God.

The so-called Lord's Prayer in Matthew 6:9-13 was given to us as a pattern for how to pray. To properly pray according to the words of this prayer, we have to stop and understand what we're saying.

"Thy kingdom come, thy will be done on earth, as it is in heaven." [v. 10]

When you say this prayer, it means you're actually praying in God's manifested presence and His kingdom so that those same heavenly principles are at work down here, the goal being that the earth would begin to look more like heaven.

THE AUTHORITY OF THE BELIEVER

When we do the ministry of evangelism, we're not fighting for victory, but from victory! We're not coming from an angle of "Golly-gee-whiz, look at all the gangs, and look at all the businessmen who don't want to hear anything about Jesus, and maybe I'm not doing any good, and maybe I'd just be better off at home watching Christian TV or eating pizza." No, He says that WE are the ones who should call the shots. *They are on our turf!* We are to enforce the victory of Calvary. That's exciting, whether it's evangelism or prayer. We've got to pray and preach with that kind of confidence.

Look at the authority God gave his servant Jeremiah:

> **Then the LORD put forth his hand, and touched my mouth. And the LORD said unto me, "Behold, I have put My words in thy mouth.**
> **See, I have this day set thee over the nations and over the kingdoms, to root out, and to pull down, and to destroy, and to throw down, to build, and to plant."** (Jeremiah 1:9-10)

The Christian is the most important and *influential* person on the earth. In light of this, just how good of a farming job have we been doing? Isn't it time we humbly and boldly take our rightful place? To be successful at farming, you must realize that God has sent you to be the farmer! (John 1:6)

Charles Finney, perhaps America's greatest evangelist, said something amazing:

> "Revival is no more miraculous than growing a crop of wheat."

Wow! Often we think that God will just sovereignly move, and he'll show up at different places if He wants, and hopefully our city is on His Top Ten list. But Finney had revivals virtually everywhere He went. He said, in so many words, *"If you want revival, learn how to farm. If you learn how to plow, if you water, you're going to have a crop."*

Here's a heavy statement: *The size of the crop is determined by how well we farm.* Think about that. This shoots down what I call "Ultra-Calvinism." Ultra-Calvinism basically says that everything is preordained, and whoever should be saved somehow will be saved, and God's going to do it all — *whatever will be, will be.* This fatalistic doctrine has probably hurt the cause of world evangelization more than any other. It invites the presumption that if someone is supposed to be saved, somehow they will, with or without our effort.

How repulsive is the notion that God's character is such that He would pick and choose who goes to heaven or hell without the individual having any choice in the matter. That would be the same as if a father had two children drowning in a lake, and by his side are two lifesavers that could be used to rescue them, but he would choose to just throw out one of them to rescue only one child. Why, such a man ought to be put in jail! No, a thousand times *no*. The God of the Bible wills that none should perish and has provided a lifesaver for every human, in the person of Jesus, and has commissioned us to throw out the lifeline to the perishing! 1 Timothy 2:4 —

Who desires all men to be saved, and to come to the knowledge of the truth.

The reason why so many are perishing in the sea of iniquity isn't because God wills it to be so, it's because we haven't learned how to throw out the lifeline effectively. The Bible says (my paraphrase), *"No, I've given you the authority and the legal right to farm this land, and the size of the crop you're going to bring in is determined by how well you farm."*

That scares and motivates me. "God, you're telling me that there are people in this world who would have been going to heaven but will end up in hell because we didn't farm well? Lord, you're telling me that people's lives could have been different, but it isn't different for them because we didn't pray?

"Yes. You're the farmer. YOU ARE the farmer."

That is sobering and humbling. We're waiting on God to do something, but He's waiting on us. We can't do God's part, but He won't do our part. He has given us legal authority to farm His land.

3

SLIDING INTO HELL

"The wicked shall be turned into hell, and all the nations that forget God."
(Psalm 9:17)

When God looks at The United States of America, how must He feel? Well-pleased? Broken? Sorrowful? Rejected? Angry?

Here is a statistical sample of what happens every day in the U.S.A. Police arrest 500 busloads of people. 5000 people try cocaine for the first time. We smoke 85,000 pounds of marijuana. We consume 15.7 million gallons of beer and ale — that's twenty-eight million six-packs of beer, enough cans to fill a baseball stadium thirty feet deep. Every evening, we drift off to sleep with the help of six dump trucks full of sleeping pills, or thirty million tablets. Every day, Americans consume 1.2 million gallons of hard liquor. Alcohol has adversely affected an estimated fifty-six million families, costing $116 billion dollars annually.

Every thirty minutes in the United States:

> 57 kids will run away
> 14 teenagers will give birth out of wedlock
> 22 teenage women will get abortions
> 685 adolescents will use some form of narcotic
> 188 young people will abuse alcohol [1]

The first drinking experience today usually occurs around age twelve! It is no longer unusual for twelve- or even ten-year-olds to have a serious alcohol-abuse problem. (Recently in my home town of Great Falls, ten-year-old kids were selling what they call Porky Pig Acid, little Porky Pig cartoons laced with acid that were being sold in schools.) By ninth grade, 56 percent have tried alcohol. By the senior year, more than nine out of ten have taken their first drink. By age eighteen, a child will have seen 100,000 beer commercials. In Detroit, a Little

League team folded because the kids were too busy selling Crack to play baseball. [2]

In 1962, the biggest problems in schools were:

- talking in class
- chewing gum
- making noise
- running in the hall
- getting out of turn in line
- wearing improper clothes
- not putting paper in the wastepaper basket.

In the mid 1990's, the top offenses in American schools:

- rape
- robbery
- assault
- burglary
- arson
- bombing
- murder
- suicide
- absenteeism
- vandalism
- extortion
- drug abuse
- alcohol abuse
- gang warfare
- pregnancy
- abortion
- venereal disease [3]

IT'S NOT MAYBERRY ANYMORE

The enemy has come in like a flood, and the hedge has come down. It is interesting to note that in 1962 our country removed prayer from our public schools, and we've seen a downward spiral ever since. The proverbial frog boiling in the beaker has been fried to a crisp, and we still haven't been moved to tears for our nation.

As reported in the magazine "Alcohol in Society," the problem of alcoholism is ever worsening because of the billions of dollars the liquor industry spends to bombard young, impressionable minds with the message that they must be frequent drinkers in order to be accepted. The three strategies are: 1) increase the number of occasions per day where drinking is the thing to do; 2) increase the percentage of those who do; and 3) position alcoholic beverages to compete with soft drinks as thirst quenchers and refreshment beverages. The strategy is working wonderfully, locking children's developing bodies into the addiction process more deeply and quickly than ever. [4] How do you think God feels about that? Matthew 18:6 —

> **"But whoso shall offend one of these little ones which believe in Me, it were better for him that a millstone were hanged about his neck, and that he were drowned in the depth of the sea."**

Many people think that America, and the corporate machines that empower this destruction of children for the sake of money, won't be judged. They think of the story in Genesis about Sodom, when God said He would spare it for ten righteous people. "Well, America has more than ten righteous! So God won't judge us."

How does God really view a nation? Look at Matthew 11:16-19 —

> **"But whereunto shall I liken this generation? It is like unto children sitting in the markets, and calling unto their fellows,**
>
> **And saying, 'We have piped unto you, and you have not danced; we have mourned unto you, and ye have not lamented.'**
>
> **For John came neither eating nor drinking, and they say, 'He hath a devil.'**
>
> **The Son of man came eating and drinking, and they say, 'Behold a man gluttonous, and a winebibber, a friend of publicans and sinners.' But wisdom is justified of her children."**

Jesus told the generation that was alive when He walked the earth, *"What am I going to do to move you people? We played happy music, and you wouldn't be joyful. We played sad music, and you wouldn't be grieved. What must be done to get you out of your stupor?!"* Matthew 11:20-24 —

> **Then began He to upbraid the cities wherein most of his mighty works were done, because they repented not:**
>
> **"Woe unto thee, Chorazin! Woe unto thee, Bethsaida! For if the mighty works, which were done in you, had been done in Tyre and Sidon, they would have repented long ago in sackcloth and ashes.**
>
> **But I say unto you, It shall be more tolerable for Tyre and Sidon at the day of judgment, than for you.**
>
> **And thou, Capernaum, which art exalted unto heaven, shalt be brought down to hell: for if the mighty works, which have been done in thee, had been done in Sodom, it would have remained until this day.**
>
> **But I say unto you, That it shall be more tolerable for the land of Sodom in the day of judgment, than for thee."**

This is very bad news, indeed. Capernaum was the city where Jesus' ministry was based. Capernaum and Bethsaida and other nearby towns saw most of Jesus' mighty works, but they didn't repent. Jesus fed 5000 men on the hillsides right outside of Capernaum. He cast devils out of people in the streets of those cities. Those were the cities where He opened blind eyes.

God's measuring rod of a nation's righteousness is not how many miracles take place in the land. *He looks at how much repentance there is, compared to how much light is given.* These cities had the light in those days. Proverbs 14:34 —

> **Righteousness exalteth a nation, but sin is a reproach to any people.**

Can you picture Jesus on the street corner preaching, **"It's going to be better for Sodom than for you on judgment day"**? Sodom was a wicked city, with mind-boggling depravity, yet

Jesus said that these cities that appeared good and moral would be even worse off in the end.

Capernaum was one of the richest cities in the world. The wheat transportation industry and the fishing industry (where Peter had his fishing business) were in Capernaum. These were nice Jewish people. They wouldn't think of doing things that Sodom did, but Jesus warned that, "*It's going to be better for Sodom than for you!*" Are we in America in the same predicament as Capernaum?

One politician said: "If God doesn't judge America in its present state, He's going to owe Sodom an apology." Are we on the brink of judgment and don't even know it? Is God trying to raise up a Jeremiah generation to preach a prophetic, evangelistic message to get people out of their stupor? God loves people so much, He loves America so much, He's going to try anything to shake us, that we might turn around before it's too late.

I am not down on America. I love America. I'm fighting for her on my knees. My hope and prayer is that God's people would become stirred to action to reverse the statistical trend. It happened before in previous centuries. During the times when America was heading the wrong way, a group of people, which included Charles Finney and John Wesley, began to get the burden of the Lord and did something with it. They helped to turn the country back to God.

We can rediscover the principles of revival that our forefathers knew, and see our country return to the Lord in our generation. This is our land, and we have been given the power and authority to establish His kingdom in the earth (Matthew 16:19). We, the church of Jesus Christ in America, are responsible and accountable for the condition of our nation. Let's awake out of our slumber and allow God to give us His burden for our country.

4

PROTESTANTS NO LONGER — JUST TANTS

It is common practice in our enlightened society to use politically-correct terminology in order to not offend sensitive people. Because the killing of unborn babies is so utterly grotesque, we use pretty language to make it sound neat and tidy and of no consequence to anyone. An unborn baby is referred to by the scientific names *fetus* or *embryo*, depending on how advanced it is. We do not kill babies in this country, we *abort fetuses*. We do not burn babies alive, we *inject a saline solution*. We do not tear them limb from limb in the womb, we *detach and remove sections of tissue from the uterus*.

WHAT'S IN A NAME?

Here is what Webster's Dictionary says, defining **fetus**:

Function: *noun*
Etymology: *Middle English, from Latin, act of bearing young, offspring; akin to Latin fetus newly delivered, fruitful —*
  : *an unborn or unhatched vertebrate especially after attaining the basic structural plan of its kind; specifically: a developing human from usually three months after conception to birth.*

According to accepted terminology, a fetus or embryo is not a baby until it is actually outside the mother's body. Apparently, it does not matter what we do to the fetus or embryo before then. "This is a free country," argues the abortionist, "and a woman has a right to choose what happens to her body."

Here is a quote from Life Services:

Life is beautiful when life is affirmed. But now, life means choice, a choice of who is wanted and who isn't. You've heard this slogan: "Every child a wanted child." Wantedness is now a criterion for deciding who lives or dies. Fifty percent of pregnancies in our country are unplanned or unwanted; *over half of those are aborted.* One abortion occurs for every three live births. Abortion is legal all nine months of pregnancy everywhere in the country, regardless of state law. Over thirty-eight million babies have been lost to abortion since it was legalized — thirty-eight million. Approximately forty percent of women will have at least one abortion.

The latest advance in helping women to neatly and legally dispose of their responsibilities, when the baby (sorry, the *fetus*) is between six and nine months along, is something called *partial-birth abortion.* In this advanced procedure, the medicine man turns the unborn child into the breech position (feet first) and pulls the child from the mother until all but the head is delivered. He or she then forces scissors into the base of the skull and inserts a catheter to suck out the child's brain.

In September 1993, Brenda Pratt Shafer, a registered nurse with thirteen years of experience, was assigned by her nursing agency to an abortion clinic. Since Nurse Shafer considered herself very pro-choice, she didn't think this assignment would be a problem. She was wrong. This is what Nurse Shafer saw:

> I stood at the doctor's side and watched him perform a partial-birth abortion on a woman who was six months pregnant. The baby's heartbeat was clearly visible on the ultrasound screen. The doctor delivered the baby's body and arms, everything but his little head. The baby's body was moving. His little fingers were clasping together. He was kicking his feet. The doctor took a pair of scissors and inserted them into the back of the baby's head, and the baby's arms jerked out in a flinch, a startle reaction, like a baby does when he thinks that he might fall. Then the doctor opened the scissors up. Then he stuck the high-powered suction tube into the hole and sucked the baby's brains out. Now the baby was completely limp. I never went back to the clinic. But I am still haunted by the face of that little boy. It was the most perfect, angelic face I have ever seen.

After our Heavenly Father's most precious creation has been viciously reduced to what *really is* a mass of tissue, the organ buyers are eagerly waiting outside the door to bid for the parts. By the way, they get more money for nine-month-old parts than for those six-month-old parts.

HOW DO YOU THINK GOD FEELS ABOUT THIS?? The Bible says that innocent blood ***cries out*** (Genesis 4:10). There is now, just in this country, the blood of over forty million innocent babies, CRYING TO GOD FOR JUSTICE !

A child is precious at any age. At conception, everything that determines a child's uniqueness is in place. Its DNA blueprint will never be duplicated. Each life is from God and has value, regardless of age. In God's economy, there is no such thing as an unwanted child. But "abortion" robs us of seeing God's plan unfold.

IT DOESN'T HAVE TO BE THIS WAY

In our nation, every day, innocent blood is being shed. We the believers have the authority, and the power, and the responsibility to change what is happening. How many more are going to have to die before we do something about it? Another two million? Forty million? Another one hundred million before we do something about this unspeakable horror?

The church, overall, does not have the revelation that believers are called to be Christian activists instead of Christian pacifists. When we see these horrors, it is our responsibility to do something. For starters, let's identify with the plight of those unborn children so that we cry out to God in agony of spirit.

There are three million cases of child abuse or molestation going on in homes in the United States! Ponder that as you drive home through your neighborhood. God has to see all of it every night. It is easy for us to think, *"Look at all these nice neighborhoods,"* while God says, "Look at the perversion going on inside these houses."

Recently, a man who was in the ministry was arrested for molesting his fourteen-year-old daughter. His wife was hurt and brokenhearted and bitter. The man was sentenced to six months, but he only served six days. Justice? The Bible says that God hates uneven balances. Proverbs 20:10 —

A false balance is abomination to the LORD: but a just weight is His delight.

Pornography is now a *nine billion dollar* business in America. There are more adult bookstores than there are McDonald's restaurants. People who have been hooked on pornography have told me that it is harder to shake than heroin. We as a nation are now pumping pornography into homes all over the world. It's as easy as a click of a mouse.

We're in trouble. There needs to be a righteous stand in our land against the workers of iniquity. Almighty God asks this question in Psalm 94:16 —

Who will rise up for me against the evildoers? or who will stand up for me against the workers of iniquity?

I'm not against loving and helping the child-molesters to be set free from their bondage, but I WANT THEM TO STOP MOLESTING CHILDREN ! It is not right to care more about the criminal than the victim. There are broken, hurting people who need to be loved and brought to church to be helped. There are also workers of iniquity against whom we must have holy anger and say, "Enough is enough!"

Jesus has both. Through us, He can go to the torn woman whose husband molested their kids, and love her so that she can be healed. Jesus can also, through us, come against the molester with a righteous word to stop it.

The fear of God is in my heart regarding our nation. Unless the church of Jesus Christ deals head-on with these issues, and quickly, we have very little time left. God *will not* sit back indefinitely as these atrocities continue on unchecked. As it has been rightly said, "All it takes for evil to reign is for good men [and women] to do nothing."

5

GOSPEL LITE
(TASTES GREAT – LESS FILLING!)

In 1987 I was a young minister, saved for several years, brand new to the Spokane, Washington area, and was very excited about getting into ministry to win the lost. I wanted some tracts and to be turned loose on the street so I could take it for the Kingdom!! One night our evangelism team was handing out tracts slap-dab in the middle of the strip joint district. And boy, did I receive an education that night!

It wasn't long before a woman with a nice hairdo, eyelashes, negligee, and high heels came over, and I handed her a tract. She viewed me as a potential customer, while I viewed her as a potential lost soul. The following conversation left quite an impression on this young country-boy preacher.

"Here ya go, ma'am. I'd appreciate it if you'd read this pamphlet in your spare time. It's got some good news in there..."

"Oh, thank you...I'm saved, filled with the Holy Ghost and speak in tongues!

"Really? This is different. You're a Christian? Hey, I've got to ask you this. Don't you work in that joint there? As a stripper, maybe?"

"Oh yeah!"

"May I ask why?"

"Hey, I need the money. It beats working at McDonalds."

As the years passed, I learned that this was not an isolated account. I could go downtown tonight in almost any American city and talk to prostitutes and have similar conversations, such as this:

"Do you know Jesus? That Jesus loves you?"

"Oh yeah, yeah I'm born again."

What??? Then they swap scriptures.

"Well, look at how Jesus forgave the prostitute. Mary Magdalene – she was a prostitute."

Unfortunately, these women forget the rest of what Jesus said in John 8:11 –

"Go and *sin no more."*

If that's not enough to get your attention, allow me to recount an experience while doing door-to-door evangelism in one of the less respectable neighborhoods of Spokane. Things were going well until we came to a house with a big pink Cadillac parked in the driveway. The conspicuous owner got out of the car and said, "Hi, how are you doing with your survey?" In the back seat sat some skimpily-dressed ladies. We started talking with him, and guess what? *He was a born-again pimp, and a tither!*

Sad to say, this is a very accurate picture of where we are spiritually in the U.S.A. Look at the following survey taken by World Challenge Ministry, based upon interviews with 3000 people chosen at random: 84% drink, 52% smoke, 52% take drugs, 66% believe in sex outside of marriage, and 82% of these people claim to be born-again Christians!

HEAVEN, WE HAVE A PROBLEM!

Hello? According to my Bible, when a person gets saved, he changes and becomes a new person in Christ, separated from the world – looks, talks, and thinks differently from before. Why is this so uncommon in America? Do we have a different Bible here? It is frightening that many Americans think they're saved, right with God when they're really not. Matthew 7:21 –

"Not every one that saith unto me, Lord, Lord, shall enter into the kingdom of heaven; but he that doeth the will of My Father which is in heaven."

Some of the statistics concerning modern evangelism are horrifying. Today, only four to eight percent of people in America who are saved in evangelical crusades are serving God after one year has passed. Let your laughter be turned into mourning as you read the following new "convert" casualty rates that the contemporary gospel has produced.

- ° A leading U.S. denomination reported that during 1995 they secured 384,057 decisions but retained only 22,983 in fellowship. They couldn't account for 361,074 supposed conversions. That's a 94 percent fall-away rate.

- ° In November 1970, a number of churches combined for a convention in Forth Worth, Texas, and secured 30,000 decisions. Six months later, the follow-up committee could find only *thirty* still continuing in their faith.

- ° In Omaha, Nebraska, a pastor of a large church said he was involved with a crusade where 1300 decisions were made, yet not even one "convert" continued in his or her faith.

- ° In the March/April 1993 issue of *American Horizon*, the national director of home missions of a major U.S. denomination disclosed that in 1991, 11,500 churches had obtained 294,784 decisions for Christ. Unfortunately, they could find only 14,337 in fellowship. That means that despite the usual intense follow-up, they couldn't account for approximately 280,000 of their "converts."

- ° A pastor in Boulder, Colorado sent a team to Russia in 1991 and obtained 2500 decisions. The next year, the team found only thirty continuing in their faith. That's a retention rate of 1.2 percent.

- ° In Leeds, England, a visiting American speaker acquired 400 decisions for a local church. Six weeks later, only two were still committed and they eventually fell away.

- ° A mass crusade reported 18,000 decisions — yet, according to *Church Growth* magazine, 94 percent failed to become incorporated into a local church.

- ° Pastor Dennis Grenell from Auckland, New Zealand, who has traveled to India every year since 1980, reported that he saw 80,000 decision cards stacked in a hut in the city of

Rajamundry, the "results" of past evangelistic crusades. But he maintained that one would be fortunate to find even eighty Christians in the entire city.

° Charles E. Hackett, the division of home missions national director for the Assemblies of God in the United States, said, "A soul at the altar does not generate much excitement in some circles because we realize approximately ninety-five out of every hundred will not become integrated into the church. In fact, most of them will not return for a second visit."

° In October 2002, Pastor Ted Haggard of New Life Church in Colorado Springs had a similar finding: "Only three to six percent of those who respond in a crusade end up in a local church—that's a problem....I was recently in a city that had a large crusade eighteen months earlier, and I asked them how many people saved in the crusade ended up in local churches. Not one person who gave his heart to Christ in that crusade ended up in the local church."[1]

Statistics such as these are very hard to find. What organizing committee is going to shout from the housetops that after a mass of pre-crusade prayer, hundreds of thousands of dollars of expenditure, preaching by a big-name evangelist, and truckloads of follow-up literature, the wonderful results that initially seemed apparent have all but disappeared? Not only would such news be utterly disheartening for all who put so much time and effort into the crusade, but the committee has no reasonable explanation as to why the massive catch has disappeared. The statistics are therefore hushed up and swept under the carpet of "discretion."[2]

We can have big meetings and bring in special groups to break bricks or play guitars, but still only four to eight percent of the people who respond are serving God a year later. Isn't the gospel the power of God unto salvation? (Romans 1:16) What happened? When you come to the a-l-t-a-r, you're supposed to leave a-l-t-e-r-ed!

Suppose I were a big beef grower in Montana, and every year ninety-two calves out of a hundred born didn't make it through the winter, and died. How many years would I be in business? How long would it take for me to realize that something was terribly wrong?

NEW AGE CHRISTIANITY

The devil has infiltrated the gospel of Jesus Christ and removed vital parts from it. He has gone after all the so-called negatives. Now we have a church with a tolerant attitude, not wanting to offend people. The spirit of this age has crept into our midst (2 Corinthians 11:4). Instead of preaching on repentance, holiness, separation from the world, and the Lordship of Jesus Christ, we've chucked those "old-fashioned" concepts for the New Version: *"God loves you. He has a great plan for you. Why don't you pray this prayer with me?"* And you're in.

The devil's hand is constantly at work to delete or corrupt many of the crucial parts of the gospel, the parts that convict and grip our hearts to bring us to true repentance and salvation. How much damage has the devil done?

Look at the next survey, taken by sociologist Jeffrey Hadden, to see how far once Bible-believing denominations have fallen. Out of 10,000 Protestant ministers, 7441 responded to the following questions:

Was Jesus born of a virgin?

60% of Methodists said no.
49% of Presbyterians said no.
44% of Episcopalians said no.
19% of American Lutherans said no.

Is the Bible the inspired Word of God?

82% of Methodists said no.
81% of Presbyterians said no.
89% of Episcopalians said no.
57% of American Lutherans said no.

Is Jesus the Son of God?

82% of Methodists said no.
81% of Presbyterians said no.
89% of Episcopalians said no.
57% of American Lutherans said no.

Was there a physical resurrection of Jesus?

51% of Methodists said no.
35% of Presbyterians said no.
30% of Episcopalians said no.
33% of Baptists said no.
13% of American Lutherans said no.

Does Satan exist?

62% of Methodists said no.
47% of Presbyterians said no.
37% of Episcopalians said no.
33% of Baptists said no.
14% of American Lutherans said no.

It looks like the devil has run his own "Just Say No" campaign. The spiritual leaders of major denominations have been convinced to say "no" to the fundamental truths of the Christian faith.

Have our Evangelical, Pentecostal, and Charismatic movements been infiltrated? The enemy doesn't come into our churches wearing a red leotard body suit with a pitchfork and horns. He comes disguised as professor, doctor, pastor, or elder so-and-so, bringing a new revelation of truth with him. 2 Corinthians 11:13-14 states it this way:

> **For such are false apostles, deceitful workers, transforming themselves into the apostles of Christ.**
> **And no marvel; for Satan himself is transformed into an angel of light.**
> **Therefore it is no great thing if his ministers also be transformed as the ministers of righteousness; whose end shall be according to their works.**

GREASY GRACE

Keeping the gospel pure was a major passion with all the apostles in the Bible. Why? They knew that without the purity and completeness of the gospel message, souls would not be saved. That is why the devil works overtime trying to "creep in unawares" to chip away at the message anywhere he can. We are warned of this in Jude 3-4 —

> **Beloved, when I gave all diligence to write unto you of the common salvation, it was needful for me to write unto you, and exhort you that ye should earnestly contend for the faith which was once delivered unto the saints.**
> **For there are certain men crept in unawares, who were before of old ordained to this condemnation, ungodly men, turning the grace of our God into lasciviousness, and denying the only Lord God, and our Lord Jesus Christ.**

Jude warns that there has come unnoticed into our midst certain teachers who have perverted the message of grace and turned it into a license to sin. This "greasy grace" message focuses mainly on the idea that grace is unmerited favor rather than the empowerment of God to live a holy life.

Titus 2:11-12 —

> **For the grace of God that bringeth salvation hath appeared to all men,**
> **Teaching us that, denying ungodliness and worldly lusts, we should live soberly, righteously, and godly, in this present world.**

Strong's Concordance defines grace as the *"divine influence upon the heart and its reflection in the life."* The false grace message has taken away critical aspects of the gospel such as the lordship of Jesus Christ, personal holiness, and separation from the world, as though they were optional in the salvation package, like options on buying a car. These ministers of the Sloppy Agape Club love to have their congregations belly-up to the pulpit to be served an ice-cold Gospel-Lite — great tasting to the flesh, but less filling to the spirit!

An encounter I had recently at a church involved a self-proclaimed Hebrew/Greek scholar. Much of his teaching involved the discrepancies he felt existed in the translation of the English Bible. His new twists of scripture always seemed to erode the message of repentance and holiness. He eventually announced that he was going to publish his own translation of the Bible. That's scary — as if to say, *"I'm going to get the Bible to say what I want, even if I have to write it myself"!*

Jude warns us that men like this will "creep in unnoticed," but it is our responsibility as discerning Christian leaders to kick the "creeps" out. What an important time to know and love the truth. The way to recognize the false is to be so familiar with the true that it is easily recognizable.

Paul warns us that the time will come when many will be deceived by false demonstrations of supernatural power, signs, and lying wonders. The only people who will not be deceived are those who have cultivated a *love for the truth* and have *embraced it* (Thessalonians 2:9-12).

The devil has been busy, indeed. He has come in as a wolf in sheep's clothing (John 10:12). The good news: I believe that God will do a major movement in the last days to restore the true gospel, in its entirety, back to His church. The need is great and the time is now. How many more false converts must we make until we realize our modern-day gospel seed is only a shell?

6

LAW 1: THE TRUE GOSPEL

How did Jesus present the gospel? Let's go back and learn from the Master Evangelist Himself. One day a rich young ruler came to Jesus in great earnest and said, "Good master, what must I do to inherit eternal life?" And what did Jesus say? *"All right, let's pray. Right now, you need to ask me to come into your heart..."* NO! The first thing He said in Matthew 19:17 was:

"Keep the commandments."

If one of us did that in a mainstream gospel church today, they would run us out.

> *"Uhmm, yes, I'm here for salvation."*
> "Good! Are you willing to do what Jesus said?"
> *"Yes!"*
> "Okay. For starters, keep the commandments."
> *"Keep the **what**?"*

Jesus said to keep them. Why? Not because we will be saved by doing so, but to expose what is in our hearts (Romans 7:7). In this case, it exposed covetousness in the heart of the rich young ruler. The Law of God is a tremendous tool that has been lost in modern evangelism. Psalm 19:7-8 —

> **The Law of the LORD is perfect, converting the soul: the testimony of the LORD is sure, making wise the simple.**
> **The statutes of the LORD are right, rejoicing the heart: the commandment of the LORD is pure, enlightening the eyes.**

Often, we are too eager to offer a remedy before the sinner sees his need. Paul the Apostle states it this way in 1 Corinthians 1:18 —

For the preaching of the cross is to them that perish foolishness; but unto us which are saved it is the power of God.

WHY DON'T THEY GET IT?

Have you ever tried to witness to someone with a lot of enthusiasm and zeal, explaining to him how "Jesus loves you soooo much that He died for you?" Isn't it discouraging how it often doesn't seem to phase the person one bit, as though it doesn't sink in no matter how passionately you try? That's because until they understand they *need* a savior, it doesn't make sense that someone would die to be their savior! It's foolishness to them. The highly successful evangelist A.B. Earle put it this way:

> "They [the sinner] must see themselves lost before they will cry out for mercy. They will not escape from danger until **they see it!**"

Romans 10:13 is a very popular and often-used scripture for winning the lost:

For whosoever shall call upon the name of the Lord shall be saved.

The word "calls" in the Greek is *epikaleo*, which means "to call upon, appeal to, or *to call upon for aid*." This implies that the person who is doing the calling sees himself in great danger and is making an urgent appeal for someone to rescue him. An example would be someone who is drowning, coming up the third and final time for air, and grasping for aid before it is too late. Has our modern-day gospel produced the type of conviction where sinners see themselves drowning in a sea of perdition and despair? If not, it is very unlikely they will cling to the life-saver with gratitude for being saved from the sea.

Romans 10:9 says:

> **That if thou shalt confess with thy mouth the Lord Jesus, and shalt believe in thine heart that God hath raised him from the dead, thou shalt be saved.**

The word that is translated as *believe* comes from the Greek *pisteo*, which means *"to rely, adhere and cling to something or someone.* The word that is rendered *believe* means more than just to give mental assent to a fact or statement. James 2:19 states:

> **Thou believest that there is one God; thou doest well: the devils also believe, and tremble.**

The devils in hell acknowledge that Jesus is the Son of God, but they are still devils! (How pathetic it is that devils have more fear of the LORD than most Christians.) To be saved, we need a different level of belief than what the devil has.

TRUE FAITH

There was once a famous tightrope walker that balanced a wheelbarrow on a high-wire above Niagara Falls. A large cheering crowd of well-wishers were waiting to greet him. Upon arrival at the other side, the daredevil said to the ecstatic crowd, "How many of you believe I can go back across the water pushing the wheelbarrow with someone in it?" The audience roared with approval. He then pointed at one of the enthusiastic fans and said, "Sir, will you get into the wheelbarrow, and we'll go across." At the moment of truth, did the excited fan really "believe" that the tightrope walker could do it? Putting his faith into action would show if he really did (James 2:17).

This is exactly the level of believing that Jesus is looking for. As Christians, we need to "rely on, adhere, and cling to" the Lord Jesus Christ to be saved. Jesus is saying to us, *"Get in the wheelbarrow — we're going for a salvation ride! Do you believe I can get you across to the other side?"* Many Americans today acknowledge that Jesus is the Savior, applaud the idea of going to Heaven, but have never gotten into the wheelbarrow of salvation. Luke 6:46—

> **And why call ye me, Lord, Lord, and do not the things which I say?**

Titus 1:16—

> **They profess that they know God; but in works they deny him, being abominable, and disobedient, and unto every good work reprobate.**

As ministers of the gospel, let's learn to preach the gospel the way Jesus and the Apostles did. They clearly showed their listeners *why* they needed to "get in the wheelbarrow" to be saved from the wrath to come.

"THERE'S NOTHING WRONG WITH ME!"

Suppose a patient visits a doctor for a checkup, and as soon as he walks into the office the physician with great enthusiasm proclaims, "I have some great news for you. A heart donor patient just died. We can give you a new heart!" At first, the patient might be startled and dumbfounded, but soon it would turn to anger. *"You haven't even examined my heart yet, so how do you know that? I feel fine! (Where did this guy graduate?)"*

The doctor's message wouldn't be great news to the patient at all. The prognosis would seem unreasonable, foolish, and at best, premature. Common sense tells us that no one in his right mind would permit heart surgery without more evaluation than this.

But suppose the doctor makes a thorough examination: x-rays, blood tests, electrocardiograph, cholesterol, and treadmill data. When the patient is called back to the office and is confronted with the documented evidence, he will probably begin to be convinced of the need for action. The worse the diagnosis, the more receptive the patient will be to hear the remedy. After viewing the evidence of the fatal disease with his own eyes, the patient will become desperate for the cure and be willing to sell all, if need be, to receive it.

Ironically, the more information we can show the patient about his heart condition, the more ready he will be for the cure. In modern evangelistic practice, we have practically gotten rid of all the bad news in order to not scare the patient away. In fact, it is the bad news that will endear the patient to the solution with unspeakable joy. That is why a revivalist like John Wesley, who literally changed the world in his day, advised his younger colleagues:

> "Preach ninety percent law and ten percent grace to the sinner."

He, as well as many of the mightily used Christian reformers, knew that if sinners could realize their true condition before God, they would quickly and wholeheartedly embrace the remedy.

This "law before grace" gospel has produced lasting fruit throughout the centuries. Charles Finney, perhaps America's greatest evangelist, preached this uncompromised gospel with remarkable results. Ministering in the 1800's, he experienced powerful moves of God in upstate New York. Whole communities came under the conviction of God. There are accounts of people riding horseback five miles away from a town that was experiencing revival, who would fall off their horses weeping profusely, coming under conviction of sin. Great numbers of converts came to Christ and the moral climate of communities was changed. Crime became so sparse in some towns that the police formed gospel choirs to sing at the revival meetings!

Twenty years after these tremendous revivals took place, a group of Finney's skeptics went to upstate New York trying to disprove the genuineness of his results. Much to their amazement, they found that over eighty percent of Finney's converts were still living for God! Compare that to the convert retain rate today of *four to eight percent serving God one year later!* Is it possible for us to learn from the past? The destinies of nations have been changed by men and women of God preaching this type of gospel.

Read the powerful words of A.W. Tozier:

> Dare we, the heirs of such a legacy of power, tamper with the truth? Dare we with our stubby pencils erase the lines of the blueprint or alter the pattern shown us in the mount? May God forbid. Let us preach the old cross and we will know the old power."

Dare we, as sincere-hearted Christians, continue to put "Smile, Jesus Loves You" Band-Aids over the patients' cancerous sores? In Jeremiah 8:11, the prophet of God brought this indictment against the spiritual leaders of his day:

> **For they** [priests, pastors, and prophets] **have healed the hurt of the daughter of my people slightly, saying, Peace, peace; when there is no peace.**

Jesus, the Master Surgeon, would take the x-ray from God's Law, show the sinner the condition of his heart, and say, *"Here is your problem. You have heart disease. If something isn't done about it, you will die. The good news is that I can give you a new heart and you will live!"*

7

THE MIRROR

Back in the good ol' days on the wheat farm, before we had a modern cushy air-conditioned tractor with a stereo, I used to have to keep those tractor doors open all day so I would not get baked. Murphy's Law ruled: no matter which direction I plowed, the dirt-filled wind blew right along with me. I would come home, look in the mirror, and be startled at my nice new tan. Sometimes I wondered if my race had changed, but then the sweat marks appeared and I realized I was still a Caucasian.

Looking into the mirror caused me to say "YIKES!!" When I knew what I looked like, I immediately searched for a way to get clean. Seeing my filthy condition in the mirror shocked me, removed all doubt that "maybe I wasn't really all that dirty," and motivated me to go to the water to get clean.

Paul states in Galatians 3:24—

> **Wherefore the law was our schoolmaster to bring us unto Christ, that we might be justified by faith.**

The law of God is our mirror or schoolmaster that reveals our need to go to the fountain of Living Water to be cleansed.

Note: Scripture does not say to take the mirror off the wall and *use it* to get clean! We are **not** saved by trying to keep the Law! Galatians 2:16—

> **Knowing that a man is not justified by the works of the law, but by the faith of Jesus Christ...for by the works of the law shall no flesh be justified.**

The famous evangelist D.L. Moody stated it well:

> "This, then, is why God gives us the Law—to show us ourselves in our true colors."

Romans 7:12–

Wherefore the law is holy, and the commandment holy, and just, and good.

THE LAW IS GOOD

Somewhere along the way, we Americans got the idea that the commandments are really a bummer, put there to keep us from having any fun. We believe the Law is old-time religion and that it went out of date with Charlton Heston and Yule Brenner! However, my Bible says that the Law is holy, just, and good because it reveals God's standard of righteousness, affirming to our conscience the difference between right and wrong (Psalm 119:128).

No wonder that the world system doesn't want the Ten Commandments posted on the walls of our schools and courtrooms. Jesus said the world hates the light and flees from it because its deeds are evil (John 3:19-20). (As a starter, I would like to see the Ten Commandments displayed on the walls of the church first.)

As Michael Brown states in his book, *The End of The American Enterprise*:

We have failed to change the world – so the world has changed us. Do the people of the world know that they are breaking God's Law when we have not lived it out and proclaimed it?

As the church goes, so goes the world. We are to be the standard-bearers on planet earth.

Some well-meaning Christian might argue, "People already know they are sinners; they don't need to be beaten over the head about it." Paul writes specifically about this point in Romans 7:7 —

What shall we say then? Is the law sin? God forbid. Nay, I had not known sin, but by the law: for I had not known lust, except the law had said, Thou shalt not covet.

In a general sense, lost humanity knows they are sinners, but through the deceitfulness of sin their hearts have become hardened to Holy Ghost conviction. Proverbs 29:1—

He, that being often reproved hardeneth his neck, shall suddenly be destroyed, and that without remedy.

I remember the first time I stole something. Little Art was about four years old, and one of my friends had a G.I. Joe. I really liked that G.I. Joe and decided to take it home with me. I hid it under my shirt and nervously went out the door, but I felt so awful when I got home that I went to my room and hid the toy in a dresser drawer.

I was convicted, and left feeling dirty and ashamed. My tender conscience had been violated by my willful act of "coveting thy neighbor's G.I. Joe." Without anyone telling me, I knew that it was wrong to steal. Romans 2:15 says:

Which shew the work of the law written in their hearts, their conscience also bearing witness, and their thoughts the mean while accusing or else excusing one another...

Even though we know the difference between right and wrong at a very early age, what happens as the years go by? Maybe a little lie here and there or taking something that isn't yours. Add to that being unforgiving toward someone who hurt you, or lusting after the pretty babes, and before long we can have an inch-thick callous over our conscience! One can become jaded by sin lurking in our members (Romans 7:5).

The Bible teaches that the way to penetrate the conscience-callous is with the Law of God. That's why Paul wrote:

I had not known sin, but by the law.

God's standard of righteousness can break through the deception and make our conscience tender before God.

Romans 7:13 —

> **Was then that which is good made death unto me?
> God forbid. But sin,** [here is what the law is for] **that it
> might appear sin, working death in me by that which
> is good; that sin by the commandment might become
> exceeding sinful.**

God's Word clearly tells us what's needed for a deep work of conviction to take place in an unbeliever's heart. It's not enough to know that one has sinned, but we need the revelation of *the exceeding sinfulness* [awfulness] *of our sin* against God.

GOD'S WORD PROVES OUT ON THE STREET

A buddy and I were ministering door-to-door when we came across a kid named Jimmy. Jimmy was really into Metallica, with purple-spiked hair and earring — not the kind of kid you would want your daughter to bring home. After coming out of his house, he agreed to take our gospel survey. One of the first questions was: "Do you believe that in the eyes of God, you've sinned?"

"Oh yeah. You bet I do. Man, last night we drank a case of beer, me and my buddy....I have a girl friend and we like to mess around....yeah, I've sinned."

At this point, using the easy-believism gospel approach, should I have said, "You admit you're a sinner? Oh good, let's pray to accept Jesus in your heart." What would have happened? I could have walked away and said, "Well, I prayed with the guy to get saved. Notch another one on my soul-winning belt." And in so doing, we would have done Jimmy a great disservice. Though he acknowledged he was a sinner and proudly so, he had no conviction of the exceeding sinfulness of it.

Instead, we used Jesus' approach and asked Jimmy if we could share something with him. He said okay. We then began to speak God's law (the right tool for the right job).

"Thou shalt not steal. Isn't God good? God doesn't want me stealing from you, Jimmy. But Jimmy, he doesn't want you stealing from me, either. That's called sin. Thou shalt not commit adultery. Jimmy, do you know what Jesus says? Jesus says that if you look at somebody with lust, you will be held accountable for adultery. Jesus says, thou shalt not bear false witness. Don't you hate it when somebody lies about you? God hates it, too. It's called *sin*."

As we went through the commandments... pretty soon this cocky kid was staring at the ground, and he was breaking. After a couple minutes of this, I said, "Jimmy, in light of God's law, and His justice, if something happened today and you died, where would you go?"

"Man, I'd go to hell."

He saw the actual condition of his heart by looking into the mirror of God's law. Now Jimmy wasn't ready to get saved, but my buddy and I left rejoicing because we broke through the wall of deception. We knew that he would go to bed every night thinking, "If I overdose, I'm going to be in hell."

What about the vast majority of Americans? Are they awakened to their true spiritual condition before God? Many national polls indicate that when people are asked the question, "If you were to die, where would you go?" nearly ninety percent answer, "Heaven, because I'm a good person." And many are deceived. Proverbs 14:12—

> **There is a way which seemeth right unto a man, but the end thereof are the ways of death.**

Unlike most Americans, Jimmy has the truth now, and God can use it to bring conviction at a deep level. The correct tool was used on him. There are millions more Jimmys out there waiting for the truth. Who is going to love them enough to tell them?

GOD'S PATHWAY TO SALVATION

God has given us a step-by-step procedure of how a person's heart is converted to Christ. 2 Corinthians 7:10—

For godly sorrow worketh repentance to salvation not to be repented of: but the sorrow of the world worketh death.

What a great scripture! How could it be any clearer? God's Word has given us His ordained pathway to salvation! Godly sorrow does a work in our heart, which brings repentance unto salvation. The key point here is the difference between godly sorrow and worldly sorrow. Often during an altar call, we see people crying and getting very emotional, but this does not necessarily mean they are repenting before God.

We can have tears from worldly sorrow because "I got caught and I'm on my way to jail. I think I'll give my life to God and see if the Big Guy upstairs can get me out of this mess." Another prevalent worldly sorrow reason people come to Christ is a business or family problem. "My spouse left me; maybe if I give this Jesus thing a try, she'll come back."

The truth of the matter is that Jesus does care about our life issues and wants to help. Hebrews 4:15 says that He is touched by the feeling of our infirmities. 1 Peter 5:7 says:

Casting all your care upon him; for He careth for you.

Jesus does care and is ready to help. However, if a sinner comes to Christ with a worldly sorrow motive, he rarely continues in the faith when trials and tribulations come his way. The Bible clearly teaches that worldly sorrow tears do not produce repentance unto salvation, but lead to [spiritual] death. *There is a big difference between seeing yourself as "unfortunate" or seeing yourself as "guilty."*

Read the words of the successful evangelist Charles Finney:

It is of great importance that the sinner should be made to feel his guilt, and not left to the impression that he is unfortunate. Do not be afraid, but show him the breadth of the Divine Law, and the exceeding strictness of its precepts. Make him see how it condemns his thoughts and life. By a

convicted sinner, I mean one who feels himself condemned
by the Law of God, as a guilty sinner...

If you have an unconverted sinner, convict him. If you
have a convicted sinner, convert him.

The great revivalists of the past all agreed that the tool
needed to move people from worldly sorrow to godly sorrow
is the Law of God.

FICKLE BELIEVERS

In America, the average lifespan of a professing born-
again Christian is four years![1] What message does that send
to heaven from our nation? "God, it sure was nice of you to
give your Son to die for me. I'll try Him for about four years
to see if my life improves; if not, then I'll be moving on. It's
been nice knowing you."

This is the horrifying fruit of a man-centered gospel. The
greasy-grace message has produced more *casualties* than
converts! The Bible warns us that if we receive the Word with
joy and gladness, when tribulation and persecution comes
our way (which Jesus promised would happen), there is a
very good chance that the "convert" will fall away from the
faith (Luke 8:13, Matthew 13:20-21).

The person who wants to "try God" to see what He can
do for him will probably not last very long in the Christian
faith. No, it's the one who says, "I've sinned against the Lord,
and I'm sorry for it." Then God says, ***"You are now set up for
salvation. Here is your solution!"***

I can almost hear someone raising an objection: "Well,
I understand scripturally what the Law of God is for, but
I didn't get saved that way. Nobody preached the Ten
Commandments to me. I came to Christ because of His love.
I was hurting and He loved me to salvation." Well, praise the
Lord! God's love is what changes us! However, when I have
talked to people with this testimony, I usually find out that
there was conviction of sin drawing them to Jesus. It just so

happened that this person might have gotten saved *in spite of* the gospel message he heard.

This has resulted in our churches now being filled with the four-to-eight percenters whose commitments to Christ remained. Their hearts were already prepared by the Holy Spirit for salvation even before the preacher spoke. But what about the other ninety-plus percent? Don't we have an obligation to them? Shouldn't we ask the same question Jesus did after healing the ten lepers and only one came back to worship Him? *"Weren't there ten of you?* **Where are the other nine?"** I don't believe that we have the right to stay in our Eight-Percent-Club church and act as though everything is all right. Surely the *true* gospel of Jesus Christ, if presented properly with anointing, can convert more than this. Romans 1:16 —

> **For I am not ashamed of the gospel of Christ: for it is the power of God unto salvation to every one that believeth; to the Jew first, and also to the Greek.**

Doesn't your heart ache for the other ninety percent that are disillusioned that they "tried Jesus" and feel it didn't work? How sad to think that the watered-down gospel that is often preached today is responsible for many of them not continuing on with Christ.

Look at what theologian Paris Reidhead says:

> When 100 years ago earnest scholars decreed that the Law had no relationship to the preaching of the gospel, they deprived the Holy Ghost in the area where their influence prevailed of the only instrument with which He had ever armed Himself to prepare sinners for grace.

If this is the function of God's Law, why has there been so little preached about it? Does the devil know something that many of us don't? Has he been busy blinding us from the truth about the Law and its usage? Have we as God's ministers become too cowardly to tell people what they don't want to hear?

Jesus said in Luke 7:47 that a person who has been forgiven much loves much. Isn't that what we as ministers of God long to see — converts that say, "I really need Jesus as my Savior. I love him so much for what He did for me. I want to live the rest of my life in such a manner as to say *Thank you, Jesus!* I will never go back to my old life."

Is it possible that part of the reason so few Christians really love much is because they never caught the revelation that they've been forgiven much? Michael Brown sums it up this way:

> Our contemporary gospel has bread complacency instead of compassion, success instead of sacrifice, prestige instead of prayer. We no longer ask what we can do for Him, but rather what He can do for us.

Where's the gratitude that we owe Him? Haven't we all been forgiven much?

Paul writes in 1 Timothy 1:8-11 —

> **But we know that the law is good, if a man use it lawfully;**
>
> **Knowing this, that the law is not made for a righteous man, but for the lawless and disobedient, for the ungodly and for sinners, for unholy and profane, for murderers of fathers and murderers of mothers, for manslayers,**
>
> **For whoremongers, for them that defile themselves with mankind, for menstealers, for liars, for perjured persons, and if there be any other thing that is contrary to sound doctrine;**
>
> **According to the glorious gospel of the blessed God, which was committed to my trust.**

THE LAW IS PART OF THE GOSPEL OF JESUS CHRIST!

Read what Charles Spurgeon (known as the Prince of Preachers) has to say concerning this.

Lower the Law, and you dim the light by which man perceives his guilt. This is a very serious loss to the sinner, rather than a gain; for it lessens the likelihood of his conviction and conversion... I say you have deprived the gospel of its ablest auxiliary [most powerful weapon] when you have set aside the Law. You have taken away from it the schoolmaster that is to bring men to Christ...they will never accept grace till they tremble before a just and holy Law. Therefore *the Law serves a most necessary and blessed purpose and it must not be removed from its place.*

We in the contemporary Christian movement continue to try to draw sinners to Christ by doing as follows. "Come to Jesus. Won't you give your heart to Him? He loves you and died on the cross for you. He wants to give you love, joy, and peace. He will make your life happy and give you what you've been looking for." Ministers gently woo sinners to the altar with the every-eye-closed-and-every-head-bowed approach. Then, as the music gently plays, the preacher asks, "Why not ask the person next to you to come with you so Jesus can make him happy?"[2] You might get unbelievers to walk the aisle to the altar with the old hymn "Just As I Am" gently playing, but without repentance that comes from Holy Ghost conviction, they will leave the altar "Just As They Were."

Without the preaching of the Law, you have an incomplete and virtually ineffective gospel! No wonder that our salvation retention rate in America is at an all-time low. The devil has convinced us to put a cork at the end of our sword. Ray Comfort, in his book *Hell's Best Kept Secret,* points out:

We try, in our evangelical zeal, to argue sinners into the Kingdom by appealing to their intellect. We attempt to scare them into heaven by '666' campaigns. We try to seduce them into the Kingdom by telling them that Jesus will make them happy. In fact, we use every method to bring people to Christ except the method God has ordained — the Law!

The Law of the LORD is perfect, converting the soul: the testimony of the LORD is sure, making wise the simple.
(Psalm 19:7)

8

FOLLOW-UP OR PROP-UP?

At a church where I was an associate pastor, one of my duties was follow-up and visitation. One Sunday morning a man came forward after the service to give his heart to Jesus. He said a sinner's prayer with me. (Unfortunately, in those early years of ministry I used the no-repentance, easy-believism approach to winning the lost.) After the prayer, I asked him if he needed a ride next Sunday. He sheepishly said, "Yah, I guess." At this point I was getting concerned.

On the following Sunday I went to pick up new-convert John. His wife answered my knock at the door. "Hi, I'm Art Neyland and I'm here to pick up John for church."

"Church? John didn't mention anything about going to church. Well, come on in and you can talk to him."

I went inside, only to find that John was nowhere in sight.

"That's strange — John was here a minute ago."

Finally, as we walked past their bedroom door, I could hear a rustling in the closet. John's wife opened the closet door, and there he was! He was being a real closet Christian, with eyes as big as a deer's caught by headlights. It was an awkward moment for us, to say the least. His excuse was that he had already made plans for the day. (Cleaning the closet, perhaps?) John didn't attend the service that Sunday, nor any other Sunday as far as I know.

THE DEAD DO NOT SEEK GOD

This story illustrates well the difference between follow-up and prop-up. I could have tried to force John into going to church, and perhaps have promised to buy him lunch afterward or some other gimmick. But as soon as I would have stopped propping him up, he would have fallen down.

A person can go to a funeral home, remove from a coffin the cadaver that is already dressed up for church, and take him to the service. The cadaver can be propped up in the pew with a hymnal in his hand, and the ushers can include him in the attendance count. There is only one problem. He is dead!

So much of what we call follow-up is really just trying to *prop-up spiritually dead people!* This is a major energy drain for a live person. As soon as the rides to church and the free lunch and the phone calls during the week stop, the dead person is gone. My experience is that when someone really gets saved he will beat you to church! When my family and I were first saved, we were at the church nearly every day: Sunday morning, Sunday night, Wednesday Bible study, Thursday men's group… We couldn't get enough. It was all so new and exciting that we absorbed it like a sponge.

Another encounter I had several years ago made me rethink my belief on follow-up. While passing through Missoula, Montana, on the way to my home in Spokane, Washington, my mother and I stopped at a restaurant, where an unbelievable divine appointment was waiting for me. As we finished the evening meal, a very prominent ministry team walked in. They were internationally known for their ministry to youth, drawing hundreds of thousands of young people to watch them put on displays of physical strength and muscle power, and just happened to be in Missoula conducting a crusade.

As they walked through the door, my face flushed and the hands got clammy. I knew this feeling all too well: God wanted me to go over and talk with them—and I was scared! (I was just a skinny guy.) I felt led to talk to them because I had been involved with their previous Spokane crusade in the area of follow-up. After all the thousands of dollars were spent to pull off the crusade and many long hours contacting and following up on the hundreds of youth that filled out decision cards, only a small handful of young people had been added to the area churches.

It is possible that the people who attended that crusade had seeds sown into them that might have taken root later. But I was grieved when our evangelism team ministered to these youths on the streets of downtown Spokane after the crusade was over. They seemed to be deceived. When I would strike up a conversation about Jesus with one of these teenagers who was using or selling drugs, he would commonly respond, "Yeah, I got saved at the youth crusade, but it really didn't do much for me. I thought it was a bunch of hype, but I liked all the cute girls."

My heart broke after hearing many similar accounts. I was troubled at how little impact the contemporary gospel message was really having. Instead of displaying the power of God, we are trying to entice the sinner by offering what the world has, and at an inferior level. Sadly, we miss the whole point: *We don't have to be like the world to win the world!* A sincere seeker will be drawn to the ways that Christianity is different from the world, rather than to the similarities.

The legendary Bible scholar A.W. Tozier addresses the issue very well:

> That evangelism which draws friendly parallels between the ways of God and the ways of men is false to the Bible and cruel to the souls of its hearers. The faith of Christ does not parallel the world; it intersects it. In coming to Christ, we do not bring our old life up onto a higher plane; we leave it at the cross. The corn of wheat must fall into the ground and die.
>
> We who preach the gospel must not think of ourselves as public relations agents sent to establish good will between Christ and the world. We must not imagine ourselves commissioned to make Christ acceptable to big business, the press, or the world of sports, or modern education. We are not diplomats but prophets, and our message is not a compromise but an ultimatum.
>
> God offers life, but not an improved old life. The life He offers is life out of death. It stands on the far side of the cross...Simply, he must repent and believe. He must forsake his sins and then go on to forsake himself.

JUST JESUS!

Isn't offering *Jesus as He is* enough to reach a lost and dying world? Do we really have to add on the gods of this world to make Christianity attractive?

Jesus Himself said, **"When I be lifted up, I will draw all men unto Me."** He didn't say, "When I be lifted up along with the contemporary gods of self, success, sports, sex, and rock 'n' roll, *then* will all men be drawn unto Me…" Things like sports, music, success, and heterosexual sex in marriage are not inherently sinful, but Jesus doesn't need to be packaged with them as an evangelistic marketing ploy.

Our evangelism team went on an outreach in Fort Lauderdale, Florida during their spring break. Hundreds of thousands of kids were "partying their brains out" on the beaches. A nationally known campus ministry was also having an evangelistic outreach at the same place. They received many more decisions for Christ than our team did, because they had a live band playing loud secular rock music and pretty girls in string bikinis handing out gospel tracts. (For a moment, I thought I wanted to get saved, too!) Do you really think this is what Jesus had in mind in Mark 16:15 when He commissioned the church to…

Go and preach the gospel to every creature… ?

The heartbreaking result of this evangelistic mixture of the holy and secular is the disillusionment of the lost. Such was the case with the street kids in Spokane, those confused youths that tried Jesus on for size but He didn't seem to fit, or at least not the way the preacher promised.

All these accounts were going through my mind as I approached the four members of this ministry team in the restaurant. I introduced myself and began to talk to the ministry's leader and founder. I mentioned how I was a part of their crusade in a previous year and was involved with follow-up on the new converts, then told him of my concerns over how few people continued on with their decisions for

Christ and the negative comments made by the youth on the streets.

What reply did this internationally-known evangelist give to all this? *"It's the church's fault! If they would have better follow-up efforts, then more would serve God."*

The alleged problem of new converts not making it with Christ has often been blamed on lack of good follow-up. This may be partly true, but it is hard to see Jesus saying to Bartholomew, *"Bart, here's a name of a guy who filled out a decision card at the Mount of Olives rally. He didn't leave a phone number, but his address is Main & Camel Drive. I haven't seen him at the meetings for several weeks. So go visit him and see if he needs a ride to the meetings..."*

It is hard to picture such a conversation between Jesus and his Disciples, because Jesus' converts *followed Him up!* Jesus told Simon Peter and Andrew: **"Follow Me, and I will make you fishers of men."** The Bible records that they immediately left their nets and *followed Him.* (Matthew 4:19)

Jesus makes that same demand on everyone who is His disciple. Jesus' converts follow Him up! Luke 9:23 —

> **And He said to them all, "If anyone will come after Me, let him deny himself, and take up his cross daily, and follow me."**

TAKING CARE OF THE SHEEP

Now, I do believe that there is a place for follow-up, and that it is scriptural. But here is the key difference: are you following-up on a sheep or a goat? We see Jesus in Matthew 18:12 leaving the ninety-nine to search out, find, and bring back the one *lost sheep.* There are times as a Christian we can become discouraged, get caught in the thickets, or be a newborn lamb that has wandered off into wolf country.

I remember hearing the heartbreaking accounts of so-called Christian cults such as the Mormons and Jehovah's Witnesses targeting new believers that got saved at crusades in Brazil and Argentina. They would be ready to "explain" to them the ways of God more thoroughly according to their beliefs. How tragic! The Bible says in 1 Peter 5:8 that we have as an adversary...

"the devil, as a roaring lion, walketh about, seeking whom he may devour..."

and he goes after the babes in Christ first. We as more mature in the faith need to protect our young.

We also, as the church of Jesus Christ, need to stand and fight for, not with, our brothers and sisters that are in a battle. We all go through trials, tribulations, and temptations and need someone to stand with us. In the words of a Christian song: "Don't shoot the wounded; one day you might be one."

Yes, there is a place for a restorational follow-up touch. In John Chapter 21 we see the biblical example of Jesus having a follow-up visit with a fallen believer. In verse 3 Simon Peter, after failing the Lord miserably in denying that he knew Him, decided to go back to his old life occupation: *"I am going fishing."* Later in the chapter, Jesus found Peter and had breakfast with him and the disciples around a campfire.

There seems to be a real non-threatening atmosphere created when you eat a meal with someone. Scripture reveals that Jesus broke bread with many people He ministered to. He even invited Himself over to their houses for dinner on occasion! After dining with Peter, Jesus continued His restoration ministry to him. Jesus asked Peter three times if he [Peter] loved Him.

It is interesting that Jesus asked Peter this question three times, in light of the fact that he had denied Jesus three times. I believe that Jesus was dealing directly with the issue, knowing it was needed for Peter's healing process. So a vital part of a successful follow-up session is addressing the real issues head-on, not skirting around them and settling for small-talk. Note also that Jesus equates Peter loving Him with feeding His sheep and lambs.

Jesus concluded the encounter by saying, ***"Follow Me."*** A successful restoration will start with a follow-up on a fallen saint, and end with the person truly following after Christ again.

That's what Biblical follow-up is all about. If we the churches will mobilize God's people to go out to the highways and hedges to bring back that which was driven away and seek out those who are lost (Ezekiel 34:1-6), we will see a tremendous harvest in our land. (If you just brought back the backsliders, you could have the largest church in town!) The church of Jesus Christ needs to once again become a field and a force: a field with respect to effectively loving, equipping, and nurturing God's sheep; a force, with respect to going out into our communities and raising up the standard of righteousness, preaching the everlasting gospel of truth in love — a mighty army. If the church can learn these principles, we will transform our nation.

9

REDISCOVERY LEADS TO REVIVAL—Part 1

Imagine this scene. Before you is a large open field with the smell of trees giving off their fragrance on a sunny summer morning. You are taking it all in, but you are not alone. Along with you are some eighteen hundred other people. Why? What is this special occasion that has brought everyone out to the meadow this early in the morning? It's because the word has gotten out around the community that a famous preacher is in town and will be speaking at 5:00 a.m.

With curiosity, you along with the others have come out to see if this preacher really has anything to say. Promptly at 5:00 a.m., a slender man of fair complexion stands up on a tree stump and begins his message. The crowd stands motionless for quite some time listening to this man sent from Heaven, as he calmly yet very descriptively exalts the holiness of God, the Law of God, the justice of God, the wisdom of His requirements, and the justice of His wrath. Then he fixes his eyes on the crowd, and with words that pierce like a saber, addresses the sinners and skeptics alike, telling them of "the enormity of their crimes; their open rebellion, their treason, and their anarchy against God." [1]

The mood grows tense, yet no one dares say a word— as if frozen in place. Next, the most unearthly experience imaginable happens. The power of God descends so mightily that you can hear gasps, sobs, and moans over the entire crowd. Then people begin to pass out all over the area, seemingly unconscious for hours. When they come to, there is a holy hush with some, and others break out into laughter and songs of joy unto the Lord.

Does this story sound too good to be true, maybe like an evangelist's fantasy? The answer is that this is a true account of what happened under the preaching of John Wesley in the

1700's. These divine visitations from God swept into the kingdom thousands of souls for the Lord and transformed our newborn nation. An eyewitness of this advent gave the reason for this visitation from heaven.

> They had received a revelation of the holiness of God, and in the light of that, they had seen the enormity of their own sin. [2]

This was the typical result of the preaching of John Wesley, George Whitefield, Jonathan Edwards, and others with similar messages.

Benjamin Franklin described the effect of Whitefield's preaching in Philadelphia during the 1700's:

> The multitude of all sects and denominations that attended his sermons were enormous...it was wonderful to see the change so soon made in the manners of the inhabitants. From being thoughtless and indifferent about religion, it seemed as if all the world was growing religious; one could not walk through a town in an evening without hearing psalms sung in different families in every street. [3]

That is our spiritual heritage as Americans!

Some argue that the present era is the most depraved time in human history, and that things are just going to continue to get worse, but God is still bigger than man's sinfulness. Here is a description of the level of darkness that prevailed in the American colonies and in England during the mid-1700's.

> The Gin Craze began in 1689, and within a generation every sixth house became a gin shop. The poor were unspeakably wretched—over 160 crimes had the death penalty! Gin made the people what they were never before: cruel and inhuman. Hanging was a daily gala event; those jerking on the ropes were watched and applauded by men, women, and children who crowded the gallows for the best view. Prisons were unimaginable nightmares; young and old, hard crook and first offender were thrown together to fight for survival.

Women were treated even worse than the men; hundreds of hardened hookers and murderesses were locked into battle over scant and rotten rations with mothers caught when forced to steal to keep their children from starving. Open sewer trenches for toilets ran through the cells; hundreds jammed together in cells made to hold a score of prisoners; rats and insects everywhere. One man took a dog into prison with him to help protect him against the vermin; the vermin killed the dog![4]

Other reports from the New England colonies claimed that rape was so rampant that ladies would not dare to go out alone at night. Gin was so morally destructive that women would sell their babies for a bottle of it. Youths were also out of control everywhere, walking the streets in gangs, partying all night, and engaging in delinquent behavior. One historian of that era commented:

"It appeared as if God had forsaken New England."[5]

The devil has used different vices over the centuries, but always with the same destructive end.

Was there any hope for the occupants of the new American colonies? Yes! God intervened and turned the society right side up. Christians who lived at that time began to get fed up with the way things were, and began to cry out to God for deliverance. Their prayers were heard, and the Almighty began to raise up men and women of God who preached with fire from heaven and converted untold thousands to the Lord.

I marvel at the harvest of souls that came into the kingdom in colonial America. Under the powerful preaching of Edwards, Wesley, and Whitefield, "...up to 50,000 souls were added to the churches"—out of a total population of 250,000.[6] There was an increase of over one hundred percent for churches and preachers during this massive revival. It justly deserves the title of "The First Great Awakening," and it all happened shortly after the early colonial settlers were wondering if God had forsaken the land. Almighty God showed up then and changed everything!

TRUE REVIVAL

Before a nation changes, people must change. Revival is, simply, awakening the dead back to life. A.W. Tozier defined revival as that which "changes the moral climate of a community." Revival is essentially a manifestation of God; it has the stamp of Deity on it which even the unregenerate are quick to recognize. Revival is a divine visitation of God upon a society!

Isaiah cried for God to intervene for his nation in 64:1-2 —

> **Oh that thou wouldest rend the heavens, that thou wouldest come down, that the mountains might flow down at thy presence,**
>
> **As when the melting fire burneth, the fire causeth the waters to boil, to make thy name known to thine adversaries, that the nations may tremble at thy presence!**

Many pastors are claiming they are having a revival in their church (usually referring to a guest speaker talking really loud and fast), but if the move of God does not radically reform the community, you haven't had revival God's way. There was once a front-page article entitled, *An Evangelical Revival Is Sweeping The Nation, But With Little Effect.* [7] This is an oxymoron. It would be like saying, "America was hit by a five-mile-wide meteor and nobody felt it"!

When the holy presence of the Lord is manifested, everyone knows it. When Almighty God speaks, everyone listens. When God's people see things as they are and intercede for the nation, God listens. (Ezekiel 9:4) Jesus said in Luke 21:36 to...

> **"watch ye therefore, and pray always...."**

Our Lord knew we wouldn't be as fervent in prayer as we need to be until we watch and see with spiritual eyes what is really going on in our land.

Another powerful example of God's people staving off divine judgment on America is from the 1800's. What is commonly known as the Second Great Awakening reversed the downward spiral of morality. After God visited the U.S.A. in the mid-1700's,

> **...there rose up a new generation that knew not the Lord**. (Judges 2:10)

Once again, morality plummeted to all-time lows. Extreme racism, slavery, drunkenness, lewdness, and mockery of God were once again commonplace in the nation. It has been reported that some ten million Africans died because of it. Africa was raped for America's prosperity. Slavery was definitely the abomination of the age.

Spirituality also plummeted to an all-time low. Logic and human rationale began to replace repentance and faith. According to one historian:

> Bible colleges became centers of skepticism; Christian students became such a minority that on some campuses they felt compelled to meet secretly."[8]

It became commonplace for students in Bible colleges to hold mock communion services and proclaim, "God is dead."

Churches were closing their doors and denominations merged in order to huddle together the few Christians that remained. Believing in Christ was scoffed at and ridiculed by those who had been "enlightened" by the new freedoms of humanistic philosophy. Almighty God was not taken off guard nor threatened by that insubordinate generation. Again, as the final hour appeared to be approaching, the Lord God began to move as His people cried out to Him for mercy.

Barton Stone, at the invitation of Daniel Boone, preached at the Cane Ridge Revival meetings which drew over 20,000 people—an incredible event for the sparsely populated frontier. Read and marvel at this recorded account of the delivering power of God in the frontier days of the early 1800's:

> Among the thousands converted was James B. Finley, who later became a Methodist circuit rider. He wrote: "The

noise was like the roar of Niagara. The vast sea of human beings seemed to be agitated as if by a storm. I counted seven ministers, all preaching at one time, some on stumps, others in wagons and one standing on a tree which had, in falling, lodged against another...Some of the people were singing, others praying, some crying for mercy in the most piteous accents, while others were shouting most vociferously. While witnessing these scenes, a peculiarly-strange sensation such as I had never felt before came over me. My heart beat tumultuously, my knees trembled, my lips quivered, and I felt as though I must fall to the ground. A strange supernatural power seemed to pervade the entire mass of mind there collected...I stepped up on a log where I could have a better view of the surging sea of humanity.

"'The scene that then presented itself to my mind was indescribable. At one time I saw at least five hundred swept down in a moment as if a battery of a thousand guns had been opened upon them, and then immediately followed shrieks and shouts that rent the very heavens."

The American Frontier was set ablaze. The Presbyterians and Methodists immediately caught fire, and then the flame broke out among the Baptists in Carroll County on the Ohio River. Great personalities emerged from this awakening. Men like Peter Cartwright, Charles Finney, and Methodist circuit riders... **The frontier was radically transformed**. Instead of gambling, cursing and vice, spirituality and genuine Christianity characterized the early westward movement. **It was God's great hour**. Revival stopped skepticism in its tracks and returned the helm of the country to the godly! [9]

Once a revival began, it was commonplace for whole communities to come underneath the conviction of God. Winkie Pratney, in his book *Revival,* referred to it as a "divine radiation zone"! One such evangelist who experienced this level of revival was Charles Finney (from the book *Power From on High*):

I think it was on the second Sunday after this when I finished preaching in the afternoon, an aged man approached and said to me, "Can you come and preach in our neighborhood? We have never had any religious meetings there." I asked the direction and the distance and made an appointment to preach there the next afternoon, Monday, at five o'clock, in their schoolhouse. I had preached three times in the village and attended two prayer meetings on Sunday, and on Monday I went on foot to fulfill this appointment.

Since the weather was very warm that day, I felt almost too weary to walk, and was greatly discouraged before I arrived. I sat down by the shade in the wayside and felt as if I was too faint to continue. I felt that, if I did, I was too discouraged to talk to the people. When I finally arrived, I found the house to be filled, and immediately started the service with a hymn. The people attempted to sing, but the horrible discord agonized me beyond expression. I leaned forward, put my elbows on my knees and my hands over my ears, and shook my head to shut out the discord which I could barely endure. As soon as they had stopped singing, I got on my knees, almost in a state of desperation. The Lord opened the windows of heaven upon me and gave me great liberty and power in prayer.

Up to this moment, I had no idea what text I should use on the occasion. As I rose from my knees, the Lord gave me this: "Up, get you out of this place; for the Lord will destroy this city" (Genesis 19:14). I told the people, as nearly as I could recollect, where they would find it and went on to tell them of the destruction of Sodom. I gave them an outline of the history of Abraham and Lot and their relations to each other, of Abraham's praying for Sodom, and Lot being the only pious man that was found in the city.

While I was doing this, I was struck with the fact that the people looked exceedingly angry at me. Many faces looked very threatening, and some of the men looked as if they were about to strike me. This I could not understand, because I was only giving them, with great liberty of spirit, some interesting sketches of Bible history. As soon as I had completed the historical sketch, I turned to them and said that I had understood they had never had any religious meetings in that neighborhood. I then applied that fact as I thrust at them with the sword of the Spirit with all my might.

From this moment, the solemnity increased with great rapidity. In a few moments, there seemed to fall upon the congregation an instantaneous shock. I cannot describe the sensation that I felt nor that which was apparent in the congregation, but the Word seemed literally to cut like a sword. The power from on high came down upon them in such a torrent that they fell from their seats in every direction. In less than a minute, nearly all the congregation were either down on their knees or on their faces or in some position prostrate before God. Everyone was crying or groaning for mercy upon his own soul. They paid no further attention to me or my preaching. I tried to get their attention, but I could not.

I observed the aged man who had invited me there as still retaining his seat near the center of the house. He was staring around him with unutterable astonishment. Pointing to him, I cried at the top of my voice, "Can't you pray?" He knelt down and roared out a short prayer, about as loud as he could holler, but they paid no attention to him.

After looking around for a few moments, I knelt down and put my hand on the head of a young man who was kneeling at my feet and engaged in prayer for mercy on his soul. I got his attention and preached Jesus in his ear. In a few moments, he seized Jesus by faith, and then broke out in prayer for those around him. I then turned to another in the same way with the same result, and then another, and another, until I know not how many had laid hold of Christ and were full of prayer for others. After continuing in this way until nearly sunset, I was forced to commit the meeting to the charge of the old gentleman who had invited me because I had to go to fulfill an appointment in another place in the evening.

In the afternoon of the next day, I was requested to hurry back to this place because they had not been able to break up the meeting. They had been asked to leave the schoolhouse to give place to the school, but they had moved to a private house nearby. There I found a number of people still too anxious and too much loaded down with conviction to go to their homes. These were soon subdued by the Word of God, and I believe all obtained a hope before they went home.

Observe that I was a total stranger in that place. I had never seen nor heard of it before that time. However, here at my second visit, I learned that the place was called Sodom by reason of its wickedness, and the old man who invited me was called Lot because he was the only believer in that place.

After that meeting, revival broke out in that old man's entire neighborhood. I have not been in that neighborhood for many years, but in 1856, I think, while laboring in Syracuse, New York, I was introduced to a minister by the name of Cross from Saint Lawrence County. He said to me, "Mr. Finney, you don't know me, but do you remember preaching in a place called Sodom?" I said, "I'll never forget it." He replied, "I was a young man. I was converted at that meeting." He was still living as a pastor at one of the churches in that county, and is the father of a principal in our school. **Those who have lived in the region can testify of the permanent results of that blessed revival.** I can only give a few words of feeble description of that wonderful manifestation of power from on high attending the preaching of the Word.

This is what could be, and I believe will be. This is normal Christianity. We, the modern Americans, are living in freak Christianity. Generations have come and gone, and we are still waiting and asking,

> **How long, Lord? Will Thou hide Thyself forever?** (Psalm 89:46a)

Lord, You've done it before. You can do it again.

10

REDISCOVERY LEADS TO
REVIVAL—part 2

We are long overdue for a real visitation from on high. Is revival some mystical, sovereign move of God that we have no part in bringing about, or are there principles of revival from God's Word that we can learn of and enter into?

Revival scholar Dick Simmons makes this statement:

> "What God does on the earth redemptively He does by invitation only!"

We are the ones who need to pray and evoke God to visit us again. Joel 2:12-14a —

> **Therefore also now, saith the LORD, turn ye even to me with all your heart, and with fasting, and with weeping, and with mourning:**
> **And rend your heart, and not your garments, and turn unto the LORD your God: for He is gracious and merciful, slow to anger, and of great kindness, and repenteth Him of the evil.**
> **Who knoweth if He will return and repent, and leave a blessing behind Him...**

God's Word clearly reveals that there are principles or spiritual laws that need to be rediscovered to experience revival. Before there is *revival*, there is *rediscovery*. Let's carefully study the revival account of Judah during the reign of King Josiah. 2 Chronicles 34:3 —

> **For in the eighth year of his reign, while he was yet young, he began to seek after the God of David his father: and in the twelfth year he began to purge Judah and Jerusalem of the high places, and the groves, and the carved images, and the molten images.**

Josiah was zealous for righteousness and for the glory of God, purging the land of idolatry, but the visitation of God was yet to happen. Josiah had commissioned the priests to put back in order God's house after years of misuse and idolatry, and as they were refurbishing the house of God…

> …Hilkiah the priest found the Book of the Law of the Lord given by Moses.
>
> Then Hilkiah answered and said to Shaphan the scribe, "I have found the Book of the Law in the house of the LORD…"
>
> Then Shaphan the scribe told the king, saying, "Hilkiah the priest hath given me a book." And Shaphan read it before the king.
>
> And it came to pass, *when the king had heard the words of the law, that he rent* [tore] *his clothes.*
>
> Then the king commanded Hilkiah…"Go, inquire of the LORD for me, and for them that are left in Israel and Judah, concerning the words of the book that is found: for great is the wrath of the LORD that is poured out upon us, because our fathers have not kept the word of the LORD, to do after all that is written in this book."
> (2 Chronicles 34:14-21)

Revival was beginning to happen! It started with someone *rediscovering* the Law of the Lord and experiencing its convicting power. An awakening of the nation's dreadful condition before God in light of His justice was starting to grip the hearts of the hearers. Josiah the King wanted to hear more about the words of warning found in the Book of the Law.

> And Hilkiah, and they that the king had appointed, went to Huldah the prophetess…
>
> And she answered them, "Thus saith the LORD God of Israel, 'Tell the man who sent you to me,
>
> Thus saith the LORD, "Behold, I will bring evil upon this place, and upon the inhabitants thereof, even all the curses that are written in the book which they have read before the king of Judah:
>
> Because they have forsaken Me, and have burned incense unto other gods, that they might provoke Me to anger… therefore My wrath shall be poured out upon this place, and shall not be quenched."

And as for the king of Judah, who sent you to enquire of the LORD, so shall ye say unto him...

"Because thine heart was tender, and *thou didst humble thyself before God, when thou heardest His words against this place...* and humbledst thyself before Me, and didst rend thy clothes, and *weep before me; I have even heard thee also,* saith the LORD.

Behold, I will gather thee to thy fathers, and thou shalt be gathered to thy grave in peace, *neither shall thine eyes see all the evil that I will bring* upon this place, and upon the inhabitants of the same." ' " So they brought the king word again.

WANTED: MODERN JOSIAHS

What an incredible intervention of a nation's destiny that took place in this encounter. The prophetess Huldah (thank God for those Holy Ghost ladies!) proclaimed that God's judgment was upon the nation of Judah, but because of Josiah's repentance He was holding back His holy wrath during the king's lifetime! (I bet the people of Judah hoped king Josiah would live a long time!) Because of Josiah's action, a whole nation was spared from the judgment of God.

The question for us today should not be, "Where is the God of Josiah," but *"Where are the Josiahs of God?"* —those special people who touch God's heart and stop His hand of impending judgment. I believe the Lord is starting to stir the hearts of these "heaven-movers" all over this nation. Here is an account of what prayer is already doing in America.

Washington, D.C., once known as the murder capital of the country, has experienced a dramatic drop in the crime rate during six years of sustained prayer. Intercession for America (IFA) says the halving of the crime rate from 1993 to 1999 coincides with concerted intercession by Christians across the country and around the world. Violent crime is down sixty percent in the area, with the number of murders dropping from 454 in 1993 to 232 last year. Burglaries declined almost seventy percent, and rapes fell by forty percent. The overall reduction was almost three times the national percentage drop. The prayer effect began in 1990, says IFA.[1]

Praise the Lord, we can make a difference! Prayer works! God moves men to pray, and prayer moves God to men. It is imperative that we learn what is God's part in revival and what is ours. We need to pray as if it all depends on God, and work as if it all depends on us. But revival God's way is even more extensive than what is currently happening in Washington, D.C. See the results of Josiah's reformation. Josiah sent for all the elders of Judah and Jerusalem and gathered all the inhabitants in the land, both great and small, and…

> …he read in their ears all the words of the book of the covenant that was found in the house of the LORD.
> And the king stood in his place, and made a covenant before the LORD, to walk after the LORD, and to keep His commandments, and His testimonies, and His statutes, with all his heart, and with all his soul…
> And he caused all that were present in Jerusalem and Benjamin to stand to it…
> And Josiah took away all the abominations out of all the countries…and made all that were present in Israel to serve, even to serve the LORD their God. And all his days they departed not from following the LORD, the God of their fathers.

Praise God, a whole nation was restored back to God! It all started with one man seeking the Lord with his whole heart.

We read of similar accounts of national revival breaking forth as a result of rediscovering the truths of God's Word. In Nehemiah 8:1-2, 8-12 we read of what took place after the rebuilding of the wall around Jerusalem.

> And all the people gathered themselves together as one man into the street that was before the water gate; and they spake unto Ezra the scribe to bring the book of the law of Moses, which the LORD had commanded to Israel.
> And Ezra the priest brought the law before the congregation both of men and women, and all that could

hear with understanding, upon the first day of the seventh month....

So they read in the book in the law of God distinctly, and gave the sense, and caused them to understand the reading.

And Nehemiah, which is the Tirshatha, and Ezra the priest the scribe, and the Levites that taught the people, said unto all the people, "This day is holy unto the LORD your God; mourn not, nor weep." For all the people wept, when they heard the words of the law.

Then he said unto them, "Go your way, eat the fat, and drink the sweet, and send portions unto them for whom nothing is prepared; for this day is holy unto our Lord: neither be ye sorry; for the joy of the LORD is your strength.

So the Levites stilled all the people, saying, "Hold your peace, for the day is holy; neither be ye grieved."

And all the people went their way to eat, and to drink, and to send portions, and to make great mirth, because they had understood the words that were declared unto them.

What an incredible scene! After completing the wall, Nehemiah and Ezra set forth to spiritually prepare the inhabitants of Jerusalem to once again be the people of God. As was the case with Josiah's reformation, we see the convicting work of the Law of God at work in hearts of the hearers...

...for all the people wept, when they heard the words of the Law.
[verse 9]

After a time of nationwide repentance with tears, great joy came upon the people as the priest of God led the way in rejoicing before their God.

Go your way...neither be ye sorry; for the joy of the LORD is your strength.
[verse 10]

So what brought about this tremendous spiritual renewal recorded in Nehemiah? Verse 8 gives us insight.

> **So they** [the priests] **read in the book in the law of God** *distinctly*, **and gave the sense, and** *caused them to understand the reading.*

The priests articulated God's truth to their hearers so they could understand and be thoroughly affected by it.

Revival starts when someone rediscovers the old truths of God's Word, and then with anointing communicates them clearly to the people. In the words of Dr. Henry H. Halley, the author of *Halley's Bible Handbook*:

> It was the finding of the Book of the Law that brought Josiah's great reformation (2 Kings 22). It was Martin Luther's finding of a Bible that made the Protestant Reformation, and brought religious liberty to our modern world. The weakness of present-day Protestantism is its neglect of the Bible which it professes to follow. The grand need of today's pulpit is simple expository preaching.

Simply put, **rediscovery precedes revival**. Isn't it about time we rediscovered the hidden laws of the harvest for our generation?

EVIDENCE OF TRUE REVIVAL

I have often heard it said that God is not going to bring revival as in the past—that He is going to do a new thing. First of all, the Bible says that there is nothing new under the sun (Ecclesiastes 1:9). In addition, why should we want anything "new" if it doesn't result in national repentance, restoration, and a drastic change of the moral climate of society?

Some ministers desire that revival would be an outpouring of signs and wonders, healings and various supernatural manifestations. I know of one pastor who believes that the next major move of God will be in the area of finances—that the wealth of the wicked will flood into the church, resulting in the Body of Christ becoming materially wealthy. This is all fine and dandy, but aren't we missing the point of the whole matter? There have been small outpourings of God's spirit over recent years in America. We have seen healings, holy laughter, slaying in the spirit, and a lot of shouting and clapping, but we haven't seen what we could have — the very thing we so desperately need in our land — revival God's way. How about seeing entire cities falling under the conviction power of the Holy Ghost, having millions soundly converted to Christ? How about seeing abortion centers closed, child molesters stopped, crime rates plummeting, the balances of justice being righted, and the oppressed being set free? Isn't this really the mission of the church in the earth today?

> **Thy kingdom come. Thy will be done in earth, as it is in heaven.**
> (Matthew 6:10)

We in America have tried everything but God's way to bring in true revival. Read the words of reproof from revivalist Leonard Ravenhill.

> Months ago the Wall Street Journal had an article on 'The Electronic Church.' The New Testament Church was not electronic, it was electrifying. The Church fresh from the Upper Room invaded the world; now the Church in the supper room is invaded by the world.
> "The New Testament Church did not depend on a moral majority, but rather on the holy minority. The church right now has more fashion than passion, is more pathetic than prophetic, is more superficial than supernatural. The church the Apostles ministered in was a suffering church; today we have a sufficient church. Events in the Spirit-controlled Church were amazing; in this day the Church is often just amusing. The New Testament Church was identified with persecutions, prisons, and poverty; today many of us are identified with prosperity, popularity, and personalities."

Let's earnestly desire the old paths, and we will see the old power.

Some contemporary theologians argue that the doctrine of the revivalist of yesteryear was rigid and restrictive. I say, let us rediscover their beliefs that we may behold their results.

Leonard Ravenhill wrote in his classic book *Why Revival Tarries*:

> Ah! brother preachers, we love the old saints, missionaries, martyrs, reformers: our Luthers, Bunyans, Wesleys, Asburys, et cetera. We will write their biographies, reverence their memories, frame their epitaphs, and build their monuments. **We will do anything except imitate them**. We cherish the last drop of their blood, but watch carefully the first drop of our own!

My brothers and sisters in Christ who hunger for the Living God, let us pour out our life blood to find and enter into the truths that the reformers held dear. I believe God has revealed, after years of diligent study, three key Laws of the Harvest that have changed nations.

The first law these great revivalists held in common was that of a *true gospel*. As discussed in chapters six and seven, they had rediscovered the powerful function of the Law of God and its convicting effect upon the heart. The second law they entered into was *travail prayer*, birthing moves of God through intercessory prayer. The third law, which is crucial in preserving the harvest, is *total discipleship*, the message of walking blamelessly before God.

These great reformers in the fashion of Josiah and Ezra found the book of the Law, rediscovered its contents, and under the unction of the Holy Spirit clearly expounded it to the people. The revivalists of yesterday are gone. Who will rise up to take their place?

11

LAW 2: TRAVAIL PRAYER— GOD'S BIG PLOW

"Grab the suitcases! Hurry up—hurry up, Art, I'm going into labor!" Janet exclaimed in desperate frustration.

Within minutes, we arrived at the hospital eagerly awaiting the birth of our first child. We expected a short stay, but it ended up as fourteen hours of intense labor.

After a while, I got impatient sitting around the hospital waiting for the grand event to take place, so I began videotaping friends who had stopped by. Finally, someone directed my attention to a poor woman over in the corner who was going into deep labor and oblivious to everything else.

"Art, turn off that stupid camera!" were the only words she could conjure up. Feeling like an idiot, I put down the camera and began the "1-2-3-4—PUSH" routine I learned in the LaMaze class. Up to that point, I'm not sure I was being the most supportive husband to Janet!

Giving birth is no easy matter. Every fiber of a woman's being is focused with incredible intensity to get the baby out. All distractions are obliviated by the task at hand. The pain and anguish are resolved once the newborn is cuddled into the arms of Mom.

Travail and birth is the most dramatic experience a woman can have. Through tears comes great joy! The same is true of prayer—the type of prayer that births revival.

PLOWING IS HARD WORK

I remember as a boy growing up on our Montana wheat farm spending countless hours on a tractor plowing the land, getting the ground ready for seeding. I recall one particular year when I plowed up some sod that had never been tilled before. Talk about hard ground! The pull on the plow was so great that it actually made the tractor's front wheels come off

the ground. (It gave new meaning to "pulling a wheelie.")
What a ride! I remember my head actually banging off the
ceiling of the cab as the tractor bounced along the rough
terrain.

Breaking up hard ground is no easy task. In light of this,
God's mandate to backslidden Israel takes new meaning
when he prophesies to the nation in Hosea 10:12 —

> **Sow to yourselves in righteousness, reap in mercy;**
> *break up your fallow ground*: **for it is time to seek the
> LORD, till He come and rain righteousness upon you.**

As it is true in the natural realm, so it is in the spiritual.
The only way to plow up the hard, fallow ground is to bring
out a REALLY big plow! The homesteaders of yesteryear
would use large-bladed plows to unroot the native sod, which
would literally turn the ground upside down. Fallow ground
actually refers to soil that at one time had been plowed up
and made amiable, but now has been left virtually untouched
and has resodded itself again to its natural state.

Though there has been much prayer offered up for
America, how much has really broken up the hard hearts of
the people? How much prayer would really qualify as fervent
and effectual (James 5:16a)?

The word "fervent" in Greek actually means to be hot as
boiling if a liquid, or glowing if a solid! (When was the last
time you were "red-hot" in prayer for our nation?) How much
of our prayer has been focused on our needs (and greeds)
instead of the well-being of others? The great majority of our
prayer time seems to be spent telling God of our concerns
instead of listening to His.

We need to once again realize the unimaginable power
and authority He has given us to break up the fallow ground
of a wayfaring nation. God Almighty has given us the
empowerment to take dominion and farm planet earth. But
we need to move past the level of prayer where our focus is,
"Hi, my name is Jimmy, I'll take all that you'll gimme," to that
of the great Scottish revivalist Duncan Campbell, who would

be found draped over a globe of the world in his private study, crying out to God, "Give me Scotland, lest I die." Or that of our Lord and Savior in the garden as He labored and embraced God's will to be accomplished, Luke 22:44—

> **And being in an agony He prayed more earnestly; and his sweat was as it were great drops of blood falling down to the ground.**

We read the fulfillment of that prayer in Isaiah 53:11-12—

> **He [Jesus] shall see of the travail of his soul and shall be satisfied: by His knowledge shall my righteous servant justify many; for He shall bear their iniquities.**
>
> **Therefore will I divide Him a portion with the great, and He shall divide the spoil with the strong; because He hath poured out His soul unto death: and He was numbered with the transgressors; and He bare the sin of many, and made intercession for the transgressors.**

PREPARATION IS THE KEY TO MANIFESTATION

Consider the account of Jesus raising Lazarus from the dead. Most readers remember the famous words of our Lord, **"Lazarus, come forth."** How many of us have a revelation of the events that led up to this miracle? —John 11: 32-39, 41,43

> **Then when Mary was come where Jesus was, and saw Him, she fell down at His feet, saying unto Him, "Lord, if thou hadst been here, my brother had not died."**
>
> **When Jesus therefore saw her weeping, and the Jews also weeping which came with her, He groaned in the Spirit, and was troubled,**
>
> **And said, "Where have ye laid him?" They said unto Him, "Lord, come and see."**
>
> **Jesus wept.**
>
> **Then said the Jews, "Behold how He loved him!"**
>
> **And some of them said, "Could not this man, which opened the eyes of the blind, have caused that even this man should not have died?"**

> Jesus therefore again groaning in Himself cometh to
> the grave...
> Jesus said, "Take ye away the stone."
> ...Then they took away the stone from the place where
> the dead was laid. And Jesus lifted up His eyes, and said,
> "Father, I thank Thee that Thou hast heard Me."
> ...And when He had thus spoken, He cried with a
> loud voice, "Lazarus, come forth."

An incredible scene took place before the eyes of those that followed Jesus, but there is more to the story than Jesus just arriving at the tomb of Lazarus and commanding him back to life. Scripture indicates that He was "prepped" for this miracle by the burdening of His spirit. Twice we read in this account He groaned in the Spirit, and was troubled.

Many Bible scholars believe that Jesus wept because of His empathy with hurting humanity. However, I believe that the troubling of Jesus' soul came from the entire situation at hand. He heard the accusations from those close to Him, accusing Him of neglect: "If thou hadst been here, my brother had not died." Jesus heard the voice of doubters: "Could not this man, which opened the eyes of the blind, have caused that even this man should not have died?" Jesus took in the whole scene and let it trouble Him. This travailing of Spirit came before the ears of our Father as a prayer that wouldn't be denied:

> "Father, I thank thee that thou hast heard me."

If the very Son of God was led by the Spirit into this type of miracle-producing prayer, how much more need we be?

ON THE EVE OF REVIVAL

Read this account from Charles Finney's autobiography on the eve of one of his greatest revivals:

> Soon after I was licensed to preach, I went in a region
> of the country where I was a total stranger. I went there at
> the request of a female missionary society located in Oneida
> County, New York. Early in May, I think, I visited the town of
> Antwerp in the northern part of Jefferson County. I stopped

at the village hotel and there learned that there were no religious meetings held in that town at that time. They had a brick meetinghouse, but it was locked up. By personal efforts, I got a few people to assemble in the living room of a Christian lady in the place, and I preached to them on the evening of my arrival.

As I walked around the village, I was shocked with the horrible profanity that I heard among the men everywhere I went. I obtained permission to preach in the schoolhouse on the next Sunday; but before that Sunday arrived, I was very discouraged and almost terrified, in view of the state of the society which I witnessed. On Saturday, the Lord applied with power to my heart the following words, addressed by the Lord Jesus to Paul: "Be not afraid, but speak, and hold not thy peace, for I am with thee, and no man shall set on thee to hurt thee, for I have much people in this city" (Acts 18:9-10). This completely subdued my fears, **but my heart was loaded with agony for the people.**

On Sunday morning, I rose early and retired to a grove not far from the village to pour out my heart before God for a blessing on the labors of the day. **I could not express the agony of my soul in words, but struggled with much groaning** and, I believe, with many tears for an hour or two, without getting relief. I returned to my room in the hotel but almost immediately came back to the grove. This I did three times. The last time I got complete relief, just as it was time to go to the meeting.

I went to the schoolhouse and found it filled to its capacity. I took out my little pocket Bible and read for my text, "God so loved the world, that He gave his only begotten Son, that whosoever believeth in him should not perish, but have everlasting life." I set forth the love of God as contrasted with the way He was treated by those for whom He gave up his Son. I charged them directly with their profanity; and, as I recognized among my hearers several whose profanity I had particularly noticed, in the fulness of my heart and the flowing of my tears, I pointed to them and said, "I have heard these men call upon God to condemn their fellow man." The Word took powerful effect. Nobody seemed offended, but almost everybody greatly melted.

At the close of the service, the amiable landlord, Mr. Copeland, rose and said he would open the meetings in the afternoon. He did so. The meetinghouse was full, and, as in the morning, the Word took powerful effect. Thus a powerful revival commenced in the village, which soon after spread in every direction.[1]

PRAYER THAT BIRTHS MOVES OF GOD

The old revivalists called it travail prayer. Isaiah 66:8 —

For as soon as Zion travailed, she brought forth her children.

Romans 8:26 states it this way:

Likewise the Spirit also helpeth our infirmities: for we know not what we should pray for as we ought: but the Spirit itself maketh intercession for us with groanings which cannot be uttered.

This is a kind of prayer which becomes so deep that words can hardly be put to it.

Travail prayer is a deeper level than praying in tongues (for all you Charismatic readers, sorry). Praying in tongues is a very powerful weapon, but it is supposed to be a springboard to help us become more focused in our prayer, to the point where we come to a level of travail.

An example of this would be the varying degrees in which light can be directed and focused. I remember as a young lad being in my grandmother's house, and the lighting always seemed so dim there. Any attempt to read a book in there would make my eyes feel like they were being pulled out of their sockets! It occurred to me that most of our prayers, including mine, are like the power of Grandma's thirty-watt bulb.

You can get more light with the same power by using fluorescent, halogen, or other modern light sources, but the ultimate is the laser, which takes light going in random directions and focuses it so intensely that it can cut through metal. The type of prayer that cuts through strong barriers is that which is focused with the burden of the Lord, coming right out of our spirit man up to God, like a laser beam. Out of this travail of our spirit, moves of God are birthed.

How do we get this "holy impregnation" of the Spirit? By taking on the burden of God's heart. Proverbs 15:3 says:

The eyes of the Lord are in every place, beholding the evil and the good.

What an incredible verse! Not only is God seeing all the noble and virtuous deeds of His people, but He beholds every evil thing that happens. He sees every person that is being raped, every child that is molested, every spouse that is beaten, every baby that is aborted. He sees the ten-year-old smoking his first joint of marijuana or taking his first hit of crack cocaine. He hears the cries of mothers for their children, and children for their mothers and fathers. He is aware of all the hurts, disappointments, offenses, loneliness, and heartaches that untold multitudes are carrying. And Almighty God is looking for someone who is after His heart to share His burden with.

I remember when God began to deal with me about this issue. I was participating in an outreach at Key West, Florida during the Fantasy Festival event. This event happens over Halloween weekend each year and draws thousands of homosexuals, as well as many that are heavily involved in the occult. This particular year, our evangelism team entered the Fantasy Festival parade which covered a twenty block parade route. When it was our turn to go before the parade judge (who was the mayor dressed in full drag), a member of our team came out of the coffin that we were carrying and preached to the parade committee.

"It is appointed for man once to die, and then the judgment. Where will you be one second after you die? It's Heaven or Hell. Repent and come to Jesus!" Needless to say, we didn't win the award for best entry, but we did make our point known!

Later that same weekend, God really began dealing with my heart about seeing our nation's condition the way He sees it. The multitude of so-called "normal" middle-class

Americans, many claiming to be born again, are out partying with the world, not being grieved by the filth and lewdness of events.

One afternoon during this festival, there was a march called "Perverts on Parade." Men wearing masks dressed in trench coats pretended to expose themselves to the audience. I recall one nice, young, middle-class family watching the parade and laughing at the perverts having fun with the audience. What they didn't see was the look of horror on their six-year-old boy's face as he viewed the sensual acts that were being displayed. For the remainder of the day I literally felt sick to my stomach, and spent much of the evening alone, having an unbearable ache in my heart.

How far we've fallen. It isn't the days of Mayberry anymore. We've become a nation that has forgotten how to blush over sin (Jeremiah 6:15). I left that outreach as a changed man. Never again would I endeavor to preach or pray without embracing God's broken heart over a wayfaring nation.

King David was a man who shared God's heart. He was defensive for God's honor in the land.

> **For they speak against thee wickedly, and thine enemies take thy name in vain. Do not I hate them, O LORD, that hate thee? And am not I grieved with those that rise up against thee? I hate them with perfect hatred; I count them mine enemies. Search me, O God, and know my heart: try me, and know my thoughts.**
> (Psalm 139:20-23)

Now I have often heard it said that we need not be trying to defend God because He's big enough to take care of Himself. Yes, God is able to defend Himself, but that misses the point. God is looking for someone to share His heart with! Those special men and women who are known as the friends of God—people who heed the heartfelt cry of the Godhead:

> **"Whom shall I send, and who will go for us?" Then said I, "Here am I; send me."**
> [Isaiah 6:8]

Read what revivalist Leonard Ravenhill says about embracing the burden of God's heart:

> Prayer in its highest form is agonizing sweat. Prayer is not just casting off a burden. It is having sense enough, and grace enough, and wisdom enough, and heart enough to ask God to share the burden of His great heart with me. By biblical definition, God has burdens that He shares: "My yoke is easy and my burden is light" (Matthew 11:30). Notice how often the Old Testament preachers talked about "the burden of the LORD"! Oh, to be a confidant of the Most Holy God! The Lord did not clothe Gideon with Himself, He clothed Himself with Gideon—the difference being that God was in the center and Gideon on the outside.

In Matthew 11:29 Jesus actually bids us to come and...

Take My yoke upon you, and *learn of me*; for I am meek and lowly in heart, and I will give you rest.

The Lord Jesus is asking us to yoke up together that we might learn of His tender heart. This is where travail prayer is birthed—prayer that originates from the holy ache of God's heart.

NO SHORTCUTS TO REVIVAL

Ravenhill, in his book *Revival God's Way*, tells of the process great intercessors go through to see revivals birthed.

> George Jeffreys, the great evangelist who shook areas of England during the 1930's, said that he prayed in English; if that seemed inadequate, he prayed in his more expressive native tongue, Welsh; if that failed, he prayed in tongues. But there is another stage—praying in the Holy Ghost. This is the highest form of prayer. It is inner groaning, it is inner grief, it is totally spiritual, and it is weakening to the flesh—but devastating to the powers of darkness. Did you ever hear anyone pray with a holy anointing that seemed to shake the place?
> Well, there is a step in prayer beyond this. It is painful to experience. Once in a little town in Wales, I witnessed a

woman travailing in prayer. It could not have been more painful and awesome had she been giving birth naturally and going down to the gates of death to bring forth life. This is what praying in the Holy Ghost is about — at least in the context of revival.

Joseph Caryl put it this way:

> "According to the **weight** of the burden that grieves us is the **cry** to God that comes from us."

How unlike most prayer today. We spend the majority of our prayer time trying to rid ourselves of all our burdens instead of welcoming His. We hope we can just "confess" revival into existence instead of birthing it. But there are no shortcuts to a true move of God. There is no such thing as a "C-section Revival!"

Evan Roberts was a man of much soul-agonizing prayer. He has been acknowledged as one of the key vessels used by God to usher in the great Welsh revival in the early 1900's. In his book, *Evangelical Awakenings*, J. Edwin Orr writes about the effects of the revival:

> With less than a score of intercessors when it burst, the churches of Wales were crowded for more than two years; 100,000 outsiders were converted, drunkenness was cut in half, many taverns went bankrupt. Crime was so diminished that judges were presented with white gloves signifying there were no cases of murder, assault, rape or robbery or the like to consider. **The police became "unemployed" in many districts.** Coal mines stopped work with transport difficulties. The pit ponies didn't understand their instructions; they couldn't recognize their owners' "cleaned-up" language!

Sometimes this sense of identification with the heart of God is awesome and terrifying. An observer of the Welsh Revival, David Matthews, said of Evan Roberts:

> "Prayer was the keynote of his tireless life. No action taken or engagement entered into was done so without definitely committing the matter to God. **His soul appeared to be saturated through and**

through with the spirit of prayer. It was the atmosphere in which he moved and lived…. whenever one looked into his face, he seemed engaged in intercession.… he asked God to give him a taste of Gethsemane…. However, the fact remains, and I am a living witness of the incident, that the prayer was answered in a terrifying way. Falling on the floor of the pulpit he moaned like one mortally wounded, while his tears flowed incessantly. His fine physical frame shook under crushing soul anguish. No one was allowed to touch him… The majority were petrified with fear in the presence of such uncontrollable grief. What did it mean?…No one doubted the transparent sincerity of the man, however mysterious the happenings."

When Evan Roberts stood before the congregation again, his face seemed transfigured. It was apparent to all he had passed through an experience that was extremely costly. No one who witnessed that scene would vote for a repetition. One wonders whether such a hallowed scene should be chronicled.[2]

This is the type of prayer that transforms nations!

DESPERATE PRAYER

I was recently at a Pastor's conference where a minister from Uganda was speaking. Their nation has seen tremendous change from the tyranny of the Idi Amin regime to the present day. The pastor from Uganda told of how this incredible transformation took place. It all was birthed out of the terrifying persecution that came to the church during that time. He gave accounts of how children would witness the execution of their parents and of horrors much too evil to speak of. The result of this onslaught of terror was that it brought the church back to its primary and principal purpose: she began to pray. Not just any type of prayer — **desperate prayer**.

The Ugandan pastor spoke of how the people would have to sneak out at night to pray in the swamps with water up their chests, so as not to be found by governmental authorities.

As they prayed and wailed out to God, He heard their cry and delivered them from all their enemies (Psalm 18:48).

Today, Uganda stands as a model of what a transformed nation can be like. Crime rates, murders, and drugs all have plummeted, and righteousness is exalted in the land. At the turn of the century, Uganda's president filled a 300,000-seat soccer stadium to publicly dedicate their nation to the LORD for the next thousand years. Not only has morality been reestablished, but God's blessing is upon the economy and ecology of the land. Praise God! And it can happen to us as well! But prayer is the key—TRAVAIL PRAYER—fervent prayer that availeth much. My prayer is that God would help us to begin to see our true condition before Him, and to become so burdened with His heart for America that we would pray desperately now—before *we* are in the swamps!

The words of Jeremiah the prophet ring true:

> **For if ye thoroughly amend your ways and your doings; if ye thoroughly execute judgment between a man and his neighbor;**
> **If ye oppress not the stranger, the fatherless, and the widow, and shed not innocent blood in this place, neither walk after other gods to your hurt:**
> **Then will I cause you to dwell in this place, in the land that I gave to your fathers, for ever and ever."**
> (Jeremiah 7:5-7)

It's up to us. We will either have revival or ruin. If we don't repent as a nation, it will be because of the church's sin of prayerlessness (2 Chronicles 7:14-20). Lord God, raise up another Evan Roberts or Charles Finney in our day, who will refuse to be denied—who will pray much like Yourself and holy prophets of old:

> **My bowels, my bowels! I am pained at my very heart; my heart maketh a noise in me; I cannot hold my peace, because thou has heard, O my soul, the sound of the trumpet, the alarm of war.**

Destruction upon destruction is cried, for the whole land is spoiled: suddenly are my tents spoiled, and my curtains in a moment.

How long shall I see the standard and hear the sound of the trumpet?

For my people is foolish, they have not known me; they are sottish children, and they have none understanding: they are wise to do evil, but to do good they have no knowledge."
(Jeremiah 4:19-22)

Heal us, Lord, and we shall be healed.
(Jeremiah 3:22)

12

BUGGY WHEAT

Matthew 28:19—
"Go ye therefore and get people saved, then forget about them."
(New Modern American Evangelical Version)

One year on our farm we had a pretty good crop, but near harvest time it started to rain, and the weather forecast said the rains would continue. We had grain bins with driers in them, so we decided to cut the wheat a little wet, put it in the bins, and hope that the driers would suck the moisture out of it. If we had gambled and waited too long, we would have started losing yield the longer the crop stayed in the field.

When wheat has a questionable moisture level, it has to be checked periodically throughout the winter to see what is happening with it. In December that year, we went to check the bin. We put in the probe and pulled it out. It was full of bugs. The wheat was still too wet, and this allowed the little critters to hatch, which then devoured the kernels from the inside. When this happens, it looks like a normal store of wheat, but only the shells remain. It still looks like wheat, but it isn't wheat anymore.

There have been occasions when a person has stepped on this kind of wheat at the top of a bin and fallen straight to the bottom and suffocated, because the empty shells could not hold the weight. To prevent this, a bin must be fumigated to rid the wheat of bugs.

ALL THAT WORK FOR NOTHING

There are many calamities that can come to a farmer, but the point is this. Every year on our Montana dryland wheat farm, we work hard. We plow it, we spray to combat weeds, and we believe God for water and for a good harvest. But even if we have a good stand of wheat and go to all the work of harvesting, loading the wheat into the trucks, and unloading the grain into the bins, we can still potentially lose the crop.

Wouldn't it be awful to work that hard all year long, and end up not having anything?

With God, it's not how we start the race, it's how we finish it. Jesus said in John 15:16—

"I am looking for fruit that remains."

When He returns, will you hear these words? *"Well started, My good and faithful servant." "Well attempted there, My good buddy."* No! He will be coming back to say, *"Well done. You finished it, and you did it well, My good and faithful servant."*

Do we really love people and care about helping them? Are the people who are getting saved really doing well and making it with God? Or are we *shooting ourselves in the foot?* Just how well are we preserving the harvest?

Out of a hundred people who sign a commitment card or pray a sinner's prayer, only four to eight are found to be in church one year later?[1] If we're farmers, and we have a hundred-bushel crop, and by the time we go to take it out of our grain bin to sell there are only four to eight bushels left, we won't be farming very long.

Out of that four to eight percent who remain, ninety-five percent of them claim to be either carnal Christians (being led by the flesh and being entangled in the world), or they're babes in Christ.[2] Translation: out of the eight who might actually stay in the grain bin, only one goes on to spiritual maturity. To me, this sounds like really buggy wheat.

George Barna, in his book *The Boiling Point*, gives us this insight into the condition of the wheat in the grain bin:

> Twenty-four percent of born-again Christians believe that when Jesus was on the earth, he committed sins. Fifty-three percent of born-again Christians believe the Holy Spirit is a symbol of God's presence in power, but is not a living entity. Thirty percent of born-again Christians do not believe that Jesus physically rose from the dead.

Twenty-six percent of born-again Christians believe that "whatever is right for your life, or works best for you, is the only truth you can know."

Twenty-four percent of born-again Christians believe that with the way things are these days, lying is sometimes necessary. Nineteen percent of born-again Christians believe that viewing pornography is a matter of taste, not morality. Sixty-eight percent of born-again Christians believe that the saying, "God helps those who help themselves" is in the Bible. Forty-seven percent of born-again Christians believe that the devil is not a living being, but is a symbol of evil.

Thirty-one percent of born-again Christians believe that if a person is generally good and does enough good things for others, he will earn a place in heaven. Twenty-three percent of born-again Christians believe that there are some sins or crimes committed that God cannot forgive. Thirty-five percent of born-again Christians don't believe that it is necessary to accept Jesus Christ as your Savior to be saved from hell.

That is some very buggy wheat! HELP!! Where is the Biblical discipleship? Jesus said to go into all the nations and teach them...

> **...to observe all that I have commanded you.**
> [Matthew 28:19-20]

With people believing as the polls indicate, what fruit will result? Proverbs 23:7 —

> **For as he thinketh in his heart, so is he.**

The results of a Roper poll indicate that most born-again Christians have fallen into more sin after their conversion than before.[3] As mentioned, recent surveys conclude that the lifespan of the average born-again experience in the U.S.A. is now four years.[4] This breaks my heart. How heaven must weep over what we've done to the Son of God and his precious blood.

There is a neighbor near our farm who is a really nice guy, but I think he missed his calling. He has a hard time getting his farming done on time. When I was home recently, I drove by our neighbor's place. Poor guy. His crop was still in the field, and he never got around to harvesting it last year. Probably the reason he didn't is because there were so many weeds all over, he must not have thought it was worth harvesting.

As I study the statistics on the American church, my heart breaks. I see the host of darkness from hell coming and looking at the crop here, and I hear laughter — not from the neighbors, but from the devil... *"Look at the crop in The United States of America, in 'God's Country.' Sure, maybe there are a few kernels of wheat here and there that are growing, but those people are probably not going to be able to preserve what little they get! Haw haw haw!"*

The good news: we can do something about it, but it's going to take good, biblical discipleship again. John 8:31-32 —

Then said Jesus, "If ye continue in My word, then are ye My disciples indeed; And ye shall know the truth, and the truth shall make you free."

13

LAW 3: TOTAL DISCIPLESHIP— WALKING BLAMELESSLY

Before we evangelize the world, we first must learn to keep and preserve what we already have. Satan would appreciate it very much if we did not.

Charles Finney, Evan Roberts, and other evangelists of previous centuries had preservation rates of over eighty percent. Decades later, people were still living for the Lord wholeheartedly. How did they do it? What did they teach their converts?

We know that they prayed and that they had a pure gospel. But here is the shocker. They never reached that high of a retention rate until they implemented another law of the harvest: the teaching of *walking blamelessly before God*.

The reason this message has been hidden is because these evangelists have been criticized for teaching Christian perfection. People get really uptight when we use that word. *"Are you saying we have to be perfect?? That can't be the message. We know we can't be perfect."* Let me ask you this: What does it mean to walk blamelessly before God?

> **For I am the LORD your God: ye shall therefore sanctify yourselves, and ye shall be holy; for I am holy..."**
> (Leviticus 11:44)

Here is the first thought that most people have, including me when I was a new Christian: *"Praise God, that's in the Old Testament. That's in the awful days when they had to try to live by **the law**, and God was saying to be holy or you're going to burn; of course, under the New Testament we don't have to live under the law, because we're under grace, and, and..."*

Let's look at 1 Peter 1:14, shall we?

> **As obedient children, not fashioning yourselves according to the former lusts in your ignorance: but as He which hath called you is holy, so be ye holy in all manner**

of conversation; because it is written, "Be ye holy; for I
am holy."

Oh no, we haven't escaped it! Even in the New Testament
He is still saying "Be holy, for I am holy." Ouch. Matthew
5:48 —

Be ye therefore perfect, even as your Father which is
in heaven is perfect.

WE HAVE TO BE WHAT?

You've *got* to be kidding me. Not only is God saying to be
holy because He is holy, but now He is saying to be perfect,
because "Your Father in Heaven is perfect." Perhaps we
should first find out what is meant by "perfect." Many try
to write this off by saying that *perfect* really means *mature*.
Unfortunately, the same Greek word which is used for our
being perfect is the same one used for God being perfect. So
if you don't want to say *perfect*, you have to read it like this:
"Be ye therefore mature, even as your Father in Heaven is mature."
Some people prefer "complete." *"Be ye complete, even as your
Father in Heaven is complete."* Do you feel relieved now? No, I
think we're still in trouble.

What, then, does God require of us? Can we really walk
blamelessly before God? Yes we can! Men of God used to
teach this, but in modern times the message has been lost.
This is why our crop has not been preserved.

If we say that we have no sin, we deceive ourselves,
and the truth is not in us.
If we confess our sins, He is faithful and just to forgive
us our sins, and to cleanse us from all unrighteousness.
If we say that we have not sinned, we make him a liar,
and his word is not in us.
My little children, these things write I unto you, that
ye sin not. And if any man sin, we have an advocate with
the Father, Jesus Christ the righteous:
And He is the propitiation for our sins: and not for
ours only, but also for the sins of the whole world.
(1 John 1:8–2:2)

This passage seems to contradict itself at first. John wrote that if we say we have no sin, we are liars, and His Word is not in us. He also said he writes these things so that we don't sin, and he doesn't want us to sin. Was John confused? How can both statements be true?

Upon careful study, it makes complete sense. When he says that "if we say that we have no sin" (referring to our sin nature) *"We deceive ourselves. If we confess our sins, He is faithful and just to forgive us our sins....If we say we have not sinned* [in the past tense], *we make him out to be a liar."*

Because of the fact that we have a sin nature due to the corrupt seed of Adam, we're going to sin, and we have sinned in the past as volitions of our will out of our old nature. In Chapter two, John changes gears:

These things write I unto you, that ye sin not.

And if any man sins (he doesn't say *when*, but *if* any man sins), he writes:

We have an advocate with the Father, Jesus Christ the righteous.

John is trying to let us know that, yes, we have a sin nature which has sinned in the past, but now **"these things write I unto you,"** so that you can get God's Word in you, you can walk in the power of grace, and you *do not have to sin.*

The Bible says we're not going to be perfect in an absolute way as God is, because He is all-knowing and all-powerful, but we can come into perfection in a moral sense. The modern church has resisted this teaching because it is thought to lay too heavy of a trip on people, when in fact it is the very thing needed to set them free.

The teaching of Christian perfection should be this: *whenever you have a free will of choice, there is no reason to not yield to do the right.*

Romans 6:13-16 —

Neither yield your members as instruments of unrighteousness unto sin: but yield yourselves unto God,

> **as those that are alive from the dead, and your members
> as instruments of righteousness unto God.**
>
> **For sin shall not have dominion over you: for ye are
> not under the law, but under grace.**
>
> **What then? Shall we sin, because we are not under the
> law, but under grace? God forbid.**
>
> **Know ye not, that to whom ye yield yourselves servants
> to obey, his servants ye are to whom ye obey; whether of
> sin unto death, or of obedience unto righteousness?**

Paul says we have choices in life. Either we can yield to
righteousness, or we can yield to sin. We have a choice, and
the choice is now weighted in our favor because of what Jesus
has done for us.

Philippians 2:12-13 —

> **...work out your own salvation with fear and
> trembling. For it is God which worketh in you both to
> will and to do of his good pleasure.**

Christ is now in us, making us desire to do His good
pleasure. It is weighted in our favor to do right! God says that
as Christians, when choices come our way, we have no excuse
and no reason to not yield to righteousness in every choice
that we have.

Suppose that I am a bad father. What if I came to my little
boy A.J. every day and told him, *"You are going to fail every
day. You will probably do something bad every minute. You can't
help but fail. You ARE a failure!"* (It hurts just to say that as
an illustration.) How would the little guy turn out? I would
probably be visiting him at the state penitentiary. That is how
people turn out under that kind of mentoring.

Instead, what if I came to A.J. and said, *"You don't have to
fail. As a matter of fact, there really is no reason for you to fail. You
can make it! You don't have to do that. You can go day after day and
not fail."* Now what will happen? He is going to do better. If
failure occurs, we will deal with it and then go on.

What I might have told A.J. as a bad father is what we tell
our new converts. Here is what typically happens today:

"Hi! We're really glad you got saved. You're still going to sin every day, because you can't help it. Every time you do, just come back to Jesus and he'll forgive you. We're just sinners saved by grace. We're going lo sin. We hope to see you in heaven."

The Bible does not say that we are *sinners saved by grace.* That is a corny saying someone came up with to make us feel better about our pitiful condition. The Bible calls us *saints.* This is not to say that we are to be self-righteous, but that God is the one who sets the standard. He puts the standard high because He now wants us to experientially become that.

Here is an important question: do you think we can go ten seconds without willfully sinning? How about twenty? How about a minute? Can we put five of those minutes together? Is that possible? (I thought we were sinners.) Can we go an hour without knowingly sinning? Two hours? Twelve hours? Incredible. That really changes the message I was taught as a new Christian. I don't have to sin every day!

Notice that Jesus, after forgiving the woman caught in adultery, didn't say, *"Go and sin a little bit every day…"* Nor did He say, *"Of course I know you sin, because My law is so hard and unreasonable; I don't really expect anyone to always obey."*[1] Jesus said, **"Go and sin no more."** If Jesus commands us to do so, it must be possible.

I believe that walking blamelessly before God works like this. Suppose you are driving your car at night with your headlights on, and suddenly a deer jumps into the road. Because you were diligent and "driving in the light," you were able to steer the car out of the way of disaster. The same holds true for walking perfectly before God. Although we are already perfect in Christ positionally, He wants us to walk it out experientially. We need to make righteous choices for the light we've been given. 1 John 1:7 tells us:

If we walk in the light as He is in the light, we have fellowship one with another, and the blood of Jesus Christ His Son cleanseth us from all sin.

Not only is our sin being cleansed when we are walking in the light of God's Word, but we are also able to see the road ahead. Psalm 119:105 —

Thy word is a lamp unto my feet, and a light unto my path.

Proverbs 16:17 states it this way:

The highway of the upright is to depart from evil: he that keepeth his way preserveth his soul.

Some may argue, "What about all the sin we do every day that we're not even aware of?" Praise the Lord, God has already made provision for it. Numbers 15:27-28 —

And if any soul sin through ignorance, then he shall bring a she goat of the first year for a sin offering. And the priest shall make an atonement for the soul that sinneth ignorantly, when he sinneth by ignorance before the LORD, to make an atonement for him: and it shall be forgiven him.

The Old Testament clearly shows us that God has made atonement for sins done in ignorance. In the New Testament, Jesus is our High Priest who has washed us clean in His own blood. Hebrews 9:13-14 says:

For if the blood of bulls and of goats, and the ashes of an heifer sprinkling the unclean, sanctifieth to the purifying of the flesh:
How much more shall the blood of Christ, Who through the eternal Spirit offered Himself without spot to God, purge your conscience from dead works to serve the living God?

Hallelujah! God through the blood of His Son Jesus has made provision for all of our sins to be atoned for, even the sins done in ignorance. We can now live life with a clear conscience, not wondering if there is some unknown sin standing between God and us!

WALKING IN THE LIGHT

This revelation of truth has helped me experience victory as never before. For years, I always felt defeated, not knowing if there was some unknown sin in my life that was displeasing to God. I thank God for the freedom that came to me when I realized that the blood of Jesus cleanses me from **all** sins, even those that I'm not aware of. Now my focus is on dealing with those sins that He is shedding light on.

Someone might think, "Why would I want any more light if I'll be held accountable for it?" Sorry, there are no loopholes with God. Proverbs 4:18 says:

> **But the path of the just is as the shining light, that shineth more and more unto the perfect day.**

God is faithful to give us more and more light if we are on the pathway of the just. We are now accountable to make right choices for the light we have. As Christians, we need to do what's right in the light! If we fail to walk perfectly before God, it's because we *would not* instead of *could not*.

The standard that Jesus set is called Freedom and Liberty. Our freedom is supposed to be from sin, rather than to sin! Galatians 5:16 —

> **For brethren, ye have been called unto liberty; only use not liberty for an occasion to the flesh, but by love serve one another.**

We are now free to do what we ought — not what we want! Jesus set the New Testament standard for us in Matthew 5.

> **"Blessed are the poor in spirit: for theirs is the kingdom of heaven.**
> **Blessed are they that mourn: for they shall be comforted.**
> **Blessed are the meek: for they shall inherit the earth.**
> **Blessed are they which do hunger and thirst after righteousness: for they shall be filled."**

We all love the Sermon on the Mount because it gives us a "warm fuzzy." But suddenly, Jesus changes direction on us. We find him preaching this, in verses 21-22:

> **"Ye have heard that it was said by them of old time, Thou shalt not kill; and whosoever shall kill shall be in danger of the judgment:**
>
> **But I say unto you, That whosoever is angry with his brother without a cause shall be in danger of the judgment: and whosoever shall say to his brother, Raca, shall be in danger of the council: but whosoever shall say, Thou fool, shall be in danger of hell fire."**

In verses 27-30, he does it again.

> **"Ye have heard that it was said by them of old time, Thou shalt not commit adultery:**
>
> **But I say unto you, That whosoever looketh on a woman to lust after her hath committed adultery with her already in his heart.**
>
> **And if thy right eye offend thee, pluck it out, and cast it from thee: for it is profitable for thee that one of thy members should perish, and not that thy whole body should be cast into hell.**
>
> **And if thy right hand offend thee, cut if off, and cast it from thee; for it is profitable for thee that one of thy members should perish, and not that thy whole body should be cast into hell."**

What is our sweet Lord doing? He had a nice little sermon going at first, talking about how the meek shall inherit the earth. Then he starts in about how we shouldn't murder, but that if we're mad at a brother without cause we're in danger of judgment. *"Oh, by the way, you've heard that you shouldn't commit adultery. But I say that if you even look at someone with lust in your eye, you have committed adultery in your heart, and it is better for you to pluck out that eyeball than to lust and go to hell."*

That's Jesus speaking, our loving Savior. He was tweaking the standard up higher. The church needs to understand this concept: under grace, we are to attain a *higher* standard of righteousness than Old Testament saints did under the law. We're not just trying to avoid committing adultery anymore. Now the standard is to not lust after people.

It is written in the Old Testament that we shouldn't murder. But Jesus said we shouldn't have unjustified anger toward our brother, or we're in danger. This is scary, and Jesus is extreme about it. He said it is better to pull eyes out and cut arms off than to not meet the standard. Then he spoke on several other topics: marriage, divorce, making an oath, what you say, and loving your enemies. He concluded the sermon by saying to **be perfect.**

This is Jesus Christ setting the new standard! The first thing we would probably say is, *"God, how do you do it? How do I make it?"* He says, "Grace. You're going to make it by grace." Not legalism. In a previous generation, some church people tried to become holy through legalistic activity. The nation then got so sick of the dry, hard-hearted, non-caring legalism that was in the 1960's, that the Jesus Movement went to the other extreme and said, "God's love is not like that. Be free, don't be under bondage, man, God's cool about everything." Because that movement went too far in the other direction, into licentiousness, where anything goes (reflected in the statistics), God is now raising up a movement where things are brought back to the center, where there is true holiness: holiness that comes through grace, not from legalism!

THE FALSE-GRACE MESSAGE

The devil has perverted the message of grace. The popular definition is "unmerited favor." I'm so tired of Christians repeating this phrase. *"Grace is unmerited favor. It's just unmerited favor."* Yes, we do not deserve grace. We do not deserve Jesus Christ dying on the cross. Granted. But they're missing the heart of grace, which is to work in us to bring us from lowliness to holiness. Grace is a vehicle to take us somewhere. Grace in Greek is *charis*, meaning *"a divine influence upon the heart and its reflection in the life."*[2]

Titus 2:11-12—

> **For the grace of God that bringeth salvation hath appeared to all men,**
> **Teaching us that, denying ungodliness and worldly lusts, we should live soberly, righteously, and godly, in this present world.**

When I run into people such as Christian bartenders, Christian pimps, or Christian strippers, and they tell me, *"It's the grace of God, brother! I'm just a sinner save by grace,"* my heart breaks. They have been deceived into a false definition of what grace is. They do not have the grace of God, because the grace of God **teaches** us to deny ungodliness and to live righteously in this present world. Instead, they have formed their own ideas of God and His grace in their minds.

I saw a picture which explained this false grace idea. It had a cardboard cutout of Jesus, and a man was standing behind the cardboard cutout drinking a beer, saying, *"He just sees Jesus – he doesn't see me."* That is the American version of the grace of God. They merely see grace as a means of covering sin, not delivering from sin. This error in belief has hurt people! It has ruined people! Look at the statistics. This wheat is full of bugs. It is destroying the contents of our grain bins. Our generation has fulfilled the prophecy of 2 Timothy 3:1-5—

> **...that in the last days...**[people will have] **a form of godliness, but denying the power thereof**.

Out of a heart of love I am now saying, *ENOUGH IS ENOUGH! THAT IS NOT THE TRUTH ABOUT GRACE !* Hebrews 12:28-29—

> **Wherefore we receiving a kingdom which cannot be moved, let us have** *grace* **whereby we may serve God acceptably with reverence and godly fear:**
> **For our God is a consuming fire.**

14

WHICH WAY ARE WE HEADED?

In June 2001, Spokane had a 3.7 earthquake. It mostly just rattled some dishes. But suppose we were warned a few hours in advance about a monster quake that was coming. Would it be smart for me to sit in my nice new car in the parking lot and pretend that I am safe, or should I leave town to avoid the danger? When the quake comes, and the ground splits open and the car and I fall in, the car won't save me. The intended purpose of the car will not have been realized. It isn't supposed to be a shrine to sit in, but a means to take me somewhere.

A woman who grew up in North Dakota told me about her dad's nice antique car. When winter came, the weather was so harsh that he would not take the car out of the garage. She actually had to walk to school when it was 40 below because good ol' Dad didn't want to take the precious car. "But Dad, you're missing the point!"

When my little boy A.J. rides his scooter across the floor, it is another picture of the grace of God. He is going from one place to another, playing with all his horns and whistles, and having fun doing it. Grace is a vehicle to take us from being a sinner to being a saint, experientially. Along the way, we do have unmerited favor, we do have blessings, and we do have gifts and callings from God. It's a package deal. It's called Grace, but *grace is supposed to be taking us somewhere.*

The love of God is this: He accepts us where we are, but loves us enough to not leave us there! Another definition of grace is "God's power to obey known truth." Jesus Christ has set the standard for Christians much higher than the Law. It is no longer just an outward act to try to keep myself from killing someone, for example. God's new standard is that, from my heart, I would love *even my enemies.* In the Old Testament, they were trying to not sleep with the cute babe who was selling camels in Jerusalem. Now God is saying, *"My standard is that you don't even lust after people. I have supplied you with the grace, the power, to do that."*

To illustrate: if you pick up a seashell on the beach, then put it up to one eye and close the other one, the little seashell blocks out the whole ocean. But if you take the shell and put it several feet away from your face, it becomes a little speck compared to the vast ocean behind it. This is how the grace of God works. When our hearts are really set on making it with God, we no longer keep looking at the Law and its standard; we begin to look at grace and who we are in Christ. Soon the issue of sin becomes small. The key to victory is being God-conscious instead of sin-conscious.

THE INVERTED GOSPEL

My heart breaks over what is happening in America. We've been doing it backwards in the church. *We've tried to get unbelievers saved by telling them the benefits of grace, and then we try to disciple the new believer by showing them the precepts of the law.* We're hurting them both ways. The new "convert" is not coming through the door of repentance for salvation, but instead is coming forward to "try Jesus, and maybe he'll give me what I want." Then when they get saved, we say, "Here is the Law. You shouldn't do this, you shouldn't do that..." We end up killing them with the wrong kind of medicine.

God wants us to rightly divide His Word again and use the right tool for the right job. 2 Timothy 2:15 —

> **Study to show thyself approved unto God, a workman that needeth not to be ashamed, rightly dividing the word of truth.**

The law is supposed to be for the sinner and the unbeliever so that they see their sin and they'll want to go to Christ for a savior. Once they decide to live for God, we shouldn't show them the Law, we should show them who they are in Christ so that they can make it! As a Christian, we are no longer a sinner having a God problem, but a godly person overcoming a sin problem! Our victory now is not a "do" but a "who." We should tell the new believer who he is in Jesus Christ. Look at the characteristics of blood-bought believers:

> Through faith, our sins are under the blood. We now live on the other side of the veil, seated with Christ in heavenly places, accepted in the beloved, one with Christ and the Father. God's wrath against our sins has been satisfied, we have been given an inheritance, we are now more than a conqueror, living and moving in the Spirit. There is no more blood line between us and Satan, our accuser has been cast down and put to an open shame, we are filled with the fullness of Christ and have a power within to meet with everything that has to do with life and godliness; we are the apple of His eye, in the hollow of His hand, purged from iniquities, reconciled, justified, sanctified, made ready as a bride, translated out of the kingdom of darkness into the kingdom of light; made an heir of all things in Christ Jesus; not under condemnation, because those who are in Christ have no condemnation; Christ abides in us and reveals himself to us. No height nor depth nor principalities nor powers, nor man, nor angels, nor things in heaven, nor things in earth, can separate us from the love of God in Jesus Christ. We are feeding on Christ the manna from heaven, living in Zion in God's presence. God is our friend, priest, advocate, Lord, and God! [1]

This is what a new believer needs. If a person doesn't know Christ, he needs to see the law ten feet tall in front of him. For a person trying to make it with God, he doesn't need the weight of the law, he needs to see God like an ocean. As we saw in Philippians, now God is working in him both to will and to do what is right.

WALKING IN VICTORY

Today, I drank all the beer I wanted to. I looked at all the porno magazines I wanted to. I had all the cigarettes I wanted to. The bottom line is: I don't want those things. I'm seated in heavenly places with Christ. I'm living in Zion in God's presence. I'm feeding off the manna of heaven, who is Jesus. I don't want the crud of the world.

A person tends to become like his mental focus. You become what you behold. (2 Corinthians 3:18) If a believer is always thinking about his sins and how far he is falling short of the standard that Jesus set, he will probably continue to do so. But when he makes Jesus his mental focus and remembers that Jesus is in those who believe, he will begin to rise to a new level without even being aware of it.

The human mind seems to be set up in such a way that the more you try not to do something, the more driven you are to do it. (Try going on a diet!) My little children A.J. and Angel put this to practice almost every time I tell them not to touch something. They may resist the temptation when Dad is watching, but as soon as I turn my back... The same is true trying to live a holy life.

I could go through the day struggling to not lust, and then this might happen: *"Oh wow, look at that gal working at the copy machine..."* Or, I can go through the day thinking the following... *"I can have fellowship with God, I can hear his voice. Lord, I want to hear your voice more, I want that joy that only comes from doing what is right, and being clean..."* When Jesus is my focus, then the next time I see the young blonde in shorts at the car shop, I'll think, *"No thanks. I'm having a nice meal of manna—why should I ruin it?"* The key to victory over the flesh is setting your mind to yield to righteousness (Isaiah 26:3-7).

Near my parents' house in Montana is a high school. One time when I went home to visit, the freshman football team was practicing. It was funny to watch those skinny little guys with the big shoulder-pads trying to be tough football players. One was trying to kick field goals. As I drove by the field, I noticed that he was so far off, the ball actually went across the road in front of my car. God showed me that, even though the kid was young and not very good at it, he had fixed his heart to try to put the ball through the uprights. Even though he was blowing it, he would get better as his heart stayed fixed.

Eventually, he would get to the point where he was kicking it through the uprights nearly every time.

This is why we are given scriptures about having a pure heart. David wrote over and over that he had fixed his heart not to sin against God. (Psalm 57:7) To quote again from Charles Finney:

> "It has been long maintained by Orthodox Divines that a person is not a Christian who does not aim at living without sin."

In other words, unless your aim is to "*go through the uprights*" to walk uprightly, unless your aim is to live without sin, you're not a Christian.

Hebrews 12:14 states it this way:

Follow peace with all men, and holiness, without which no man shall see the Lord.

The very name of Jesus literally means, "He shall save his people from [not in] their sins." (Matthew 1:21) Here is a comment on Finney from a man who studied his life and ministry:

> "The key to Finney's high retain rate of converts is his instruction on Christian perfection....that they would keep the right goal before their eyes."

How different from today!

A.W. Tozier wrote:

> "The Christian ideal is not happiness, but holiness."

Happiness is all about pleasing me; holiness is all about pleasing Him.

When it becomes my goal to live without sin, in holiness, I find something better than happiness: I find joy. Unspeakable joy comes with righteousness — the beauty of holiness. (Hebrews 1:9)

From Finney:

"Our inquiry should not be on how we feel, but what end we live for, which is the aim of our life."

According to this great man of God, our goal must be to live without sin, or we aren't Christians. But this sinlessness is obtained by being God-conscious, not sin-conscious.

The church has wrestled with many potentially conflicting concepts throughout its history, and the doctrine of holiness has always been one of them. These conflicts need to be resolved so that we can see clearly our aims and plan-of-attack. We have seen what the standard is. The purpose of God's grace is to help us attain to that standard. There are blessings, favor, and gifts from God as we go on our journey up to the standard of Zion. We can do it! As Christians we are fighting from victory, not for victory!

2 Corinthians 7:1 —

Having therefore these promises, dearly beloved, let us cleanse ourselves from all filthiness of the flesh and spirit, *perfecting holiness* in the fear of God.

15

WHO'S THE ENEMY?

If we have all these great and wonderful promises given us to live a holy and victorious life (see 2 Peter 1:3-4), why are so few Christians experiencing it? The Bible warns us of three formidable enemies we face each and every day: the devil, the flesh, and the world system. 1 John 2:15—

> Love not the world, neither the things that are in the world. If any man love the world, the love of the Father is not in him.
>
> For all that is in the world, the lust of the flesh, and the lust of the eyes, and the pride of life, is not of the Father, but is of the world.
>
> And the world passeth away, and the lust thereof: but he that doeth the will of God abideth for ever.

Our challenge is this. The Bible says that we should not be ignorant of the devil's devices. (2 Corinthians 2:11) We must remember that the devil doesn't come to us head-on. He doesn't show up in the red leotard suit with the pitchfork and say, *"Hey-hey-hey! Here's a beer!"* We'd say, "Wait—aren't you the devil, the one who is trying to make me go to hell?"

The devil prefers subtlety. He disguises himself by showing up in the world system, which is the lust of the flesh, the lust of the eyes and the pride of life. *"It looks good, it feels good, and it's all for you!"* This is how most marketing works, trying to appeal to our flesh so that we will buy the latest products. That's the voice of the devil working through this world system. What is his purpose in doing that? He is trying to get you to have an affair with the world, and cheat on God.

We're not going to finally break free from the things that entangle us and be able to go up to Zion, to the standard, until we learn how to not be enticed by the world. We need to see the world for what it is. It's not just a good time; it's not just the sleek lady on a billboard selling you a bottle of whiskey.

(They don't show you the wino with no teeth who just vomited on himself).

So what is the devil trying to do? He's trying to lure us. And it's more than just alcohol, immoral sex, and all the obvious things. He wants to harden our hearts and take away our affection toward the Lord. Hebrews 3:13 —

> **Take heed, brethren, lest there be in any of you an evil heart of unbelief, in departing from the living God.**

SATAN WANTS YOU TO HAVE AN AFFAIR ON GOD

It is something like a soap opera, with God wanting to be our lover. Here is the fickle human who sort of wants to be with God, but as soon as the world shows up, she suddenly wants to have a fling with him. After a time of being beaten up by the world, she says, *"Oh, but God was so nice, I want to go back to God now. Oh yes, I love you, Lord, you know, you're really the one I want to be with."* Then when the dashing young lover comes back into town: *"Well, now I'm getting bored,"* and right away she's back over with the world.

God finally had enough of this in James 4:4 —

> **Ye adulterers and adulteresses, know ye not that the friendship of the world is enmity with God? Whosoever therefore will be a friend of the world is the enemy of God.**

In other words: *"If you are a friend with the world, you are My enemy — you are whoring on me."* This breaks God's heart. Exodus 34:14 says that God's name is *Jealous*. God's a jealous God. It is good that He is jealous over us, as though married to us. *"I don't want you to cheat on me. I'm jealous with a godly jealousy."*

2 Peter 3:10-12 —

> **But the day of the Lord will come as a thief in the night; in the which the heavens shall pass away with a great noise, and the elements shall melt with fervent heat, the earth also and the works that are therein shall be burned up.**

Seeing then that all these things shall be dissolved, what manner of persons ought ye to be in all holy conversation and godliness,

Looking for and hasting unto the coming of the day of God, wherein the heavens being on fire shall be dissolved, and the elements shall melt with fervent heat?

There is a day coming when all the world will be burned up. It's all going to burn. Zephaniah 3:8 says:

Therefore wait ye upon me, saith the LORD, until the day that I rise up to the prey: for My determination is to gather the nations, that I may assemble the kingdoms, to pour upon them mine indignation, even all My fierce anger: for all the earth shall be devoured with the fire of My jealousy.

Here is a scripture about Armageddon. At the end of our time as we know it, *"I'm going to gather together all the ungodly people who didn't want Me and My Son. I will then pour out My wrath and burn up the earth."* This fire is not just an indifferent, inanimate object. *It is actually a manifestation of the jealousy of God.* God is going to burn up the world system, because the world was the adulterous lover to mankind.

NO CHEATING ALLOWED

In 1981 a dear friend of mine became a Christian. Shortly after his conversion, something terrible happened: his wife ran off with the marriage counselor of the church. This was not a nice way to start out his Christian walk. The day it happened, we had planned to go to a ball game. I came into his house and found him sitting in his chair, physically going into shock. He hardly knew what had happened. His skin felt ice-cold, and I had to put blankets on him. *"She left me"* is all he could say. I heard him call his adulterous wife. He talked to her about coming back, and there was a brokenness. *"I love you and I want you back, but you can't just go out and cheat on me."*

When I saw that, God gave me the revelation that this is how He feels. Jesus is a broken-hearted lover because mankind is whoring on Him. They're having an affair with the world. This is God's heart toward lost humanity: *"I want you back, but you have to stop being unfaithful to Me!!"*

As his evangelists and His messengers, we need to convey this message: " *"God wants you back, and He's broken-hearted, but you cannot keep cheating on Him."* Many do not understand that even though Jesus is trying to draw people back to Him, there is coming a day when the time will be up. When this happens, He will come back to the earth as an enraged lover, to torch it, out of jealousy—the world and those who have chosen to be adulterous against Him.

Shortly after moving to Spokane, I was preparing to minister on the street one day. I was sitting at an outdoor espresso bar, and God spoke to my heart and said, *"Art, you're not going to be effective in being My mouthpiece in reaching this city until you learn how not to love all the things of the world that are around you."*

Now, God's not against us having nice things or a good time. It's not what we have that concerns God, but what has us! God is not going to use vessels which have not become separated, because that lack of separation keeps us from having His heart. As His evangelists, we need to see His standard. The victory and the joy are realized when we live at that standard. He wants us to see that the true grace of God will help us do that. He wants us to keep our eyes on who we are in Christ, and what the good news is for his saints. At the same time, we are to learn to hate the adulterous lover.

Jude 23—

> **And others save with fear, pulling them out of the fire; hating even the garment spotted by the flesh.**

When we're ministering in a city, and go to a beach where the women are wearing less than what I normally have on my wrist, I cannot allow myself to stare at the beach babes. This would take me out of the anointing and defeat the entire purpose of being there.

Love not the world, nor the things that are in the world.

To be effective, we have to separate ourselves from sin. It won't really happen until we see it for what it is, and what it does to our Lord and Savior. A.W. Tozier put it this way:

A person hasn't truly repented until they realize that it was their sin that crucified Christ.

I want to walk uprightly before God because I love Him and appreciate what He has done.

What if someone asked me, "Art, you can marry the dream lady of your life, but you have to let her cheat on you with her old boyfriend once a week." No thanks! Even though I love her, *no thank you*. Because I love her, no thank you. What if I were to let her do that once a month? Just once a month she gets to go with her old boy friend, and the other 29 days I can be with her. *No thank you!* What about once a year? Once a year I let her have a little wild fling, and the rest of the time she's mine. *NO THANK YOU!!*

Do we love Jesus like that, like a pure, devoted bride? I want to. I want to be in that process of saying, *"Lord, I want to be that holy, spotless bride."* Jesus really is coming back for a holy and pure bride (Ephesians 5:27). This is not just positional truth; it is experiential as well. He is looking for a people who love Him so much that they choose not to yield to unrighteousness. For every free will choice I have, I can say, *"Lord, I'm going to do what brings You the greatest glory, and love my neighbor as myself."* (Matthew 22:37-40). And the spirit of God is in me, saying *"Yessss!! Do it."*

Unless your aim as a Christian is to live without sin, then you must have a heart adjustment. You need spiritual surgery to get your heart fixed. Once this kind of message is proclaimed, where we 1) see God's standard and how provision has been made for us to live there, 2) know the great truths of who we are in Christ, and 3) get a hatred for the world system, thatfour to eight percent retention rate will begin to improve. It will happen when these truths become a part of us and when we impart them to others.

Take heed unto thyself, and unto the doctrine; continue in them: for in doing this thou shalt both save thyself, and them that hear thee.
(2 Timothy 4:16)

16

THE LAST STRAW

Farmers in southern Alabama were once accustomed to planting one crop every year: cotton. They would plow as much ground as they could and plant their crop. Year after year they lived by cotton.

Then one year the dreaded boll weevil devastated the whole area. So the next year the farmers mortgaged their homes and planted cotton again, hoping for a good harvest. But as the cotton began to grow, the insect came back and destroyed the crop, wiping out most of the farms.

The few who survived those two years of the boll weevil decided to experiment the third year, so they planted something they'd never planted before: peanuts. And peanuts proved so hardy, and consumers were so ravenous for that product, that the farmers who survived the first two years reaped profits that enabled them to pay off all their debts. They planted peanuts from then on and prospered greatly.

Then the farmers spent some of that new wealth to erect in the town square a monument — to the boll weevil! If it hadn't been for the boll weevil, they would never have discovered peanuts. They learned that even in a disaster there can be great discovery. [1]

It's been said that the last seven words of a dying church are, *"We've never done it this way before."* Christianity in America has steadily declined for the past fifty years. According to David Roozen and C. Kirk Hardaway in their book, *Church and Denominational Growth,* U.S. churches have failed to gain an additional two percent of the American population. As a matter of fact, the western world is the only major segment of the world's population in which Christianity is not growing. Consider these growth trends from various parts of the world:

- Worldwide, Christianity is growing at the rate of 90,000 new believers every day.
- The church in Africa is increasing by 20,000 per day, average.
- More Muslims in Iran have come to Christ since 1980 than in the previous thousand years combined.
- In 1900, Korea had no Protestant church; it was deemed "impossible to penetrate." Today, North/South Korea are 35 percent Christian, with 7000 churches in the city of Seoul alone.
- After 70 years of oppression in Russia, people who are officially Christians number about 85 million—56 percent of the population.
- Every day in India, 15,000 people become Christians.
- 3000 new churches are opening every week worldwide.[2]

Praise God for what He is doing across the globe! How tragic in light of this are the statistics of North America:

- Almost three times as many churches in America are closing (3750) as are opening (1300) each year.
- In terms of faith groups here on American soil, every other religion is gaining converts, while Christianity is losing them. [Islam is growing so fast in the United States that it threatens to surpass Judaism as the second largest religious group.]
- The world's largest Muslim training center is in New York City.
- Buddhism is growing nearly three times as fast as Christianity.
- The largest Buddhist temple in the world is in Boulder, Colorado.
- The world's largest training center for Transcendental Meditation is in Fairfield, Iowa.
- Roughly half of all churches in America did not add one new person through conversion growth last year.
- Statistics reveal that it takes the combined efforts of eighty-five Christians working over an entire year to produce one convert. [At that rate, a huge percentage of people will never have the opportunity, even once, to hear the gospel

from a friend they trust and in a way they can understand.][3]

North America may have been the perceived leader of Christianity in past decades, but no one can make a case for that today. Many leading sociologists have labeled America as a "post-Christian nation." Statistics depicting moral conditions would prove the conclusion to be accurate.

According to Tom Clegg and Warren Bird in their book "Lost in America," the United States leads the industrialized nations in these categories:

- Single parent families (at 23 percent)
- Abortion rate (at 22.9 per 1000 women ages 15-44)
- Sexually transmitted diseases (syphilis rate 6.3 per 100,000; gonorrhea rate 149.5 per 100,000)
- Teenage birthrate (42 per 1000 girls ages 15 - 19)
- Use of illegal drugs by students (44.9 percent in 1998)
- Size of prison population (327 per 100,000)
- Rate of child poverty (20 percent). *[Abysmal!]*

Clegg and Bird conclude their findings by stating:

Where is the church's positive impact on individuals and society? At stake is the deadly assumption that business as usual is just fine. It's even more deadly when churches aren't even aware that they've made such an assumption. We impact one life here and another one there, and we wrongly assume that as other churches do likewise, we're making forward progress.

The exact opposite is true. Churches are going out of business. Why? Because they refuse to change. They're like the proverbial frog placed in a slowly warming pot of water. The frog gets cooked because it doesn't notice and doesn't respond to the changes around it.

Any church that doesn't shift from "ministry as status quo" to "ministry as mission field" will die or it becomes hopelessly irrelevant to the people its charter document — the Bible — calls it to love, serve, reach, and even die for."

My purpose in writing this book is not to just point out the bleak problems of America and its church, but to offer a viable solution. Albert Einstein was credited with defining stupidity as *"doing the same thing repeatedly, expecting a different result."*

IT'S TIME FOR A CHANGE!

Let's go back to what once worked and pick up where great men and women left off. Jeremiah the prophet cried out with the voice of reason to the inhabitants of backslidden Jerusalem in his day:

> **Thus saith the Lord, "Stand ye in the ways, and see, and *ask for the old paths*, where is the good way, and walk therein, and ye shall find rest for your souls." But they said, "We will not walk therein."**

My hope and prayer is that we will have a better response to the mandate from God than did the backslidden Israelites — who eventually saw the judgment of God fall on their land.

After fifteen years of study on the topics of evangelism and revival, I believe God has opened my eyes to three essential keys for revival. What did great men and women of God have in common that were mightily used by the Lord, not only to start revivals but to sustain them as well?

1.   They knew how to pray! They birthed moves of God through travail prayer.

2.   They all had a gospel that brought conviction at a deep level.

3.   They preached and taught their converts in the way of holiness — walking blamelessly before God.

Smith Wigglesworth, the apostle of faith; John G. Lake, the mightily-used healing evangelist; William Seymore, the spark that was used to start the Azusa Street Revival — all were devout followers of John Wesley's beliefs of holiness and entire consecration to God.

William and Catherine Booth, the founders of the Salvation Army that brought massive revivals and social reformation to England in the 1800's; Jeremiah Lamphere, the businessman that was instrumental in the 1857 revival in New York City; George Williams, an English worker, that started the YMCA as an evangelistic outreach to youths—all were strongly influenced by Charles Finney's teachings on revival, as were many others.

Often in history, countries have plummetted into gross immorality and unbelief, but God still prevailed triumphantly. Where sin abounds, grace much more abounds (Romans 5:20). What is needed is not a **miracle**, but a **man or woman** who says, "Enough is enough!" The key is to see the need for change and to be determined to do something about it!

Consider the account of Gideon. (Judges 6:6-14)

> **And Israel was greatly impoverished because of the Midianites; and the children of Israel cried unto the LORD.**
>
> **And it came to pass, when the children of Israel** *cried* **unto the LORD because of the Midianites, that the LORD** *sent* **a prophet unto the children of Israel...**
>
> **And the angel of the LORD appeared unto him** [Gideon] **and said unto him, "The LORD is with thee, thou mighty man of valour."**
>
> **And Gideon said unto him, "Oh my Lord, if the LORD be with us, why then is all this befallen us? And where be all his miracles which our fathers told us of, saying, 'Did not the LORD bring us up from Egypt?' But now the LORD hath forsaken us, and delivered us into the hands of the Midianites."**
>
> **And the LORD looked upon him, and said, "Go in this thy might, and thou shalt save Israel from the hand of the Midianites:** *have I not sent thee***?"**

We are waiting on God to move, and He is waiting on us. God wants us to cry out for deliverance, so He can send a deliverer! How much more has to take place in our nation before we rise up to stop the devil from ransacking this generation? What more must happen before we cry out as the Israelites: "Where is the God of our forefathers and why hast thou forsaken us"?

When will we realize that what we are doing **isn't working?** Yes, we do have some great churches in the land, and there are men and women doing wonderful works for the Lord—but the bottom line is, we are losing our nation! We will either have revival or ruin! **Isn't it time to change our farmin'?**

The good news is: one person can make a difference! One man or woman armed with the truth, empowered by the Spirit, can change the world, not only in their lifetime but for generations to come. One person and God make a majority! John Wesley proclaimed:

> "Give me one hundred men who fear nothing but sin, and desire nothing but God, and I will shake the world."

Revival never happens by accident. Someone has to pay, and pray, the price. Who will be that person in our day? You are as close to God right now as you want to be. The reason we don't have revival in America is because we think we can live without it. How badly do we want it?

Tradition is always the challenger to truth; one or the other must go. We **can** have revival, but we dare not deviate from the pattern shown us on the mount. As leaders, we need to show the way. Let's not compromise and give the people what they want, when it is well within our grasp to give them what they need. The next move is ours. Jeremiah 23:22—

> **But if they [spiritual leaders] had stood in My counsel, and had caused thy people to hear My words, then they should have turned them from their evil way, and from the evil of their doings.**

ENDNOTES

PREFACE

1.Tom Clegg & Warren Bird, *Lost in America* [Group, 2001], 113.

CHAPTER 3

1. Stephen Anterburn & Jim Burns, *Drug Proof Your Kids* [Focus on the Family, 1989], 11.
2. Ibid, 12.
3. David Wilkerson, *The Final Purge* [tape].
4. Stephen Anterburn & Jim Burns, *Drug Proof Your Kids* [Focus on the Family, 1989], 12.

CHAPTER 5

1. Kirk Cameron & Ray Comfort, *The Way Of The Master* [Tyndale House Publishers, Inc., 2002], 61-63.
2. Ibid, 63.

CHAPTER 7

1. John Muncy, *Matters of the Heart* (audio tape sermon).
2. Ray Comfort, *Hell's Best Kept Secret* [Whitaker House, 1984], 14.

CHAPTER 9

1. Ray Comfort, *Hell's Best Kept Secret* [Whitaker House, 1984], 72.
2. Ibid 72.
3. Winkie Pratney, *Revival* [Whitaker House, 1984], 112.
4. Winkie Pratney, *Revival* [Whitaker House, 1984], 70-71.
5. Ibid, 112.
6. Ibid, 313.
7. Leonard Ravenhill, *Revival God's Way* [Bethany House, 1986], 56.
8. Winkie Pratney, *Revival* [Whitaker House, 1984], 121.
9. Ibid, 125-126.

CHAPTER 10

1. Tom Clegg & Warren Bird, *Lost in America* [Group 2001], 111.

CHAPTER 11

1.Charles Finney, *Power From on High* [Whitaker House, 1996], 21-24.
2. Winkie Pratney, *Revival* [Whitaker House, 1984], 305-306.

CHAPTER 12

1. Kirk Cameron & Ray Comfort, *The Way of the Master* [Tyndale House Publishers, Inc., 2002], 61-63.
2. Leonard Ravenhill, *Revival God's Way* [Bethany House, 1986], 56.
3. Michael L. Brown, *Whatever Happened to the Power of God* [Destiny Image, 1991], x.
4. John Muncy, *Matters of the Heart* [audio tape sermon].

CHAPTER 13

1. Jed Smock, *Who Will Rise Up?* [Hunting House, 1985], 146.
2. Strong's Concordance.

CHAPTER 14

1. David Wilkerson, *God's Intention For This Midnight Hour* (tape).

CHAPTER 16

1. Craig Brian Larson, *750 Engaging Illustrations* [Baker Books, 2002], 17.
2. Tom Cleg & Warren Bird, *Lost in America* [Group, 2001], 26.
3. Ibid, 22, 30-31.